UNCONDITIONAL
EXCELLENCE

UNCONDITIONAL EXCELLENCE

ANSWERING GOD'S CALL TO BE YOUR PROFESSIONAL BEST

by
Alan M. Ross
and Cecil Murphey

Adams Media Corporation
Avon, Massachusetts

Published by
Adams Media Corporation
57 Littlefield Street, Avon, MA. USA.
www.adamsmedia.com

ISBN: 1-58062-706-4

Printed in the United States.

J I H G F E D C B

Library of Congress Cataloging-in-Publication Data
is available from the publisher.

This publication is designed to provide accurate and authoritative information with
regard to the subject matter covered. It is sold with the understanding that the publisher is not engaged in rendering legal, accounting, or other professional advice. If
legal advice or other expert assistance is required, the services of a competent professional person should be sought.
—From a *Declaration of Principles* jointly adopted by a Committee of the American
Bar Association and a Committee of Publishers and Associations

The illustrations in this book are true. For the sake of privacy, whenever I use only a
first name, this indicates that I altered a few facts, such as the gender or name.

Many of the designations used by manufacturers and sellers to distinguish their
products are claimed as trademarks. Where those designations appear in this book
and Adams Media was aware of a trademark claim, the designations have been
printed in initial capital letters.

This book is available at quantity discounts for bulk purchases.
For information, call 1-800-872-5627.

Dedication

I dedicate this to all employees who quietly and consistently go about their daily work with Unconditional Excellence. They are truly the bright lights in dark places that honor their God.

Acknowledgments

To my wife, Sara, and to our sons, Patrick and Michael, who continue to encourage, challenge, and love me unconditionally.

My special thanks to my cowriter, Cecil ("Cec") Murphey, who exemplifies Unconditional Excellence in all he does.

Both of us wish to acknowledge Gary Krebs, Director of Publishing, and his staff. Their passion for *Unconditional Excellence* challenged us to make this book all that it was intended to be. The wisdom, guidance, and painful honesty were invaluable to the process.

Contents

chapter one

The Legacy of Unconditional Excellence

If I told you I had a secret formula that would guarantee you a successful career, what would you pay to get it? Suppose I said, "Memorize this formula, apply it every day, and you will be totally successful." Would you be willing to use that formula? At least give it a reasonable trial?

The answers are obvious.

This book, however, is not about a secret formula. I offer no guarantee of career success. However, I do offer secret *principles*, and if you *apply* them to your life, they can lead to success in your career. Please notice the two words I've stressed. I can give you the secret principles, but you must apply them.

Now is the time for two disclaimers—the principles aren't really secrets, because they've been known and have been around for centuries. They're secrets in the sense that they're commonly overlooked or misunderstood. They're also secrets in that few people who yearn for success live by them. Yes, the principles are well known—and that may be part of the problem. They're widely known; they just aren't widely practiced.

I also want to say that just being successful in business and in my personal life isn't enough—at least it isn't for me. I want more than success. I also want peace of mind, an inner assurance that I've lived a worthwhile life, and the knowledge that I've helped others in their quest to live better lives.

The Principle

Everything I want to say in this book is based on one concept that I call *Unconditional Excellence*. If you learn and apply the maxims presented in the following chapters, you may not end up as king (or queen) of the hill, but you'll enjoy your life much more. You'll enjoy it because you'll know—and so will those around you—that you are a person who lives by sound precepts and is recognized for your integrity.

For several years I've shared these principles with employees at every level in corporations and among a variety of industries. I've watched people adopt these truths. I've received great satisfaction from the many stories and testimonies I've heard about the impact these principles have had on companies, leaders, customers, and—ultimately—on those who work with people of outstanding achievement. The impact the maxims have had on those who apply them brings me great joy and personal satisfaction.

In one sense, this book is my life's work. Not that I am finished with my life, but I strongly believe that my purpose is to call people in the marketplace to the concept of unreservedly giving themselves to being the best they can be. An ever-increasing passion for me is to help companies and individuals within those companies to stand out for their superior quality of people, products, and services. The best way I can do that is to challenge people in those companies to understand and embrace the principles of Unconditional Excellence. When they start living by these precepts, all the other things slowly fall into place, such as acceptance, recognition, integrity, and peace of mind.

In this quest, we need practical tools that can help us to attain the best we're capable of doing. That's what much of this book is about.

Unconditional Excellence begins when we make a choice to commit ourselves to becoming the very best in our workplace. Although it starts with a decision, it requires action—persistent, relentless, ongoing action. Too often, I've encountered people who agree with what I teach, but who don't always practice these tenets in the tyranny of the business world.

In fact, I admit that I can talk better about these precepts than I can live them. One of my great fears has always been that, after I explained everything I know, I wouldn't measure up as one who has fully put those concepts into practice. At one time I thought that if I pursued these insights with the goal of following them completely, I'd be about as perfect as any human could be and that my life and business would also reach that level.

It just doesn't work that way.

I've given up on reaching the goal of perfection. I couldn't make it anyway, but that's not the real reason. One day I realized that perfection wasn't the ultimate aim. There is an ultimate purpose—Unconditional Excellence—and that is what I strive for, because I know that's what provides the satisfaction I seek.

What Is Unconditional Excellence?

Being good enough in what we do in the workplace is not good enough; it's also not excellence.

Being better than what our job requires still isn't good enough, and it's still not excellence.

Being the best is what we aim for. That is not only excellence, but it is the one thing worth achieving.

I'm not willing to settle for anything less than being the best—the best I can be when I throw my energies and talents into any task. I want to be able to say with pride, "I stand for giving my best." I want to set a high standard and then consistently perform to that standard.

Some may pull back from saying such things about their work, accuse me of boastfulness, and urge me to be a little more humble in my approach. Someone told me I ought to say, "I try. I do what I can."

I don't agree with that, even though it's true. Trying isn't enough. Instead, it's time for those of us who believe in the principles of unreserved quality to stand up and say loudly and proudly, "I have committed myself to do my best without reservation. I offer no excuses and no apologies if I don't fully live up to my commitment."

I also want to make it clear that I don't advocate competing with others and acting as if we're saying, "Hey, I'm better than Marvin because I've done more (or earned more, or have a bigger house, or play golf more often)." I do advocate a strong determination to strive for personal, total self-commitment at every level in our work and in our personal character.

I also add a subprinciple that underlies what I've already said: Great accomplishments are not realized by people of mediocrity but by people of unreserved commitment. That means that as long as we settle for mediocrity, we'll never achieve our best.

Maybe that's obvious, but I wonder.

For myself and ultimately for my employees, I continue to move the standard of expectations higher and higher. What is at the top? Where is the pinnacle of performance we can expect to attain in this life?

Great companies are not made up of employees of average ability and acceptable performance but of employees committed to and living out lives of superior achievement and the highest ethical standards. The great discovery is that these are principles that Jesus of Nazareth taught thousands of years ago. The apostles Peter, John, and Paul and the Gospel writer Luke lived by them and taught them. Yet too often we have relegated them to our Sunday religion. God gave these principles to become the core of our lives. They transcend what we call our religion or being religious. I have no use for a list of rules. They're the mechanistic lists that claim, "If you follow these eight successive steps and pray along the way, everything will work out."

I teach core values—the essential truths and eternal principles—that God gave to the human race to enrich us individually and to build true community with others.

Tools and Skills

In this book, I share practical tools. Those who are willing to use these tools will increase their competency in what I call the applied skills. Our technical competency depends on our specific career needs, of course, but our applied skills cross over into every career, regardless of what it is. The applied skills can transform us from being a good employee into an unreservedly superior one.

Downsizing and Employability

One result of learning those skills is that those who seek Unconditional Excellence increase their employability. I have had the terrible experience in my career of downsizing a number of companies. The term *downsize* is the consultants' polite way of saying, "We need to get rid of large numbers of employees."

I have orchestrated such downsizing; I have also been through it as a corporate leader. I have learned from these experiences that even those employees who are conscientious and outstanding may lose their jobs. If the company directive says, "Downsize everyone who was hired in the past two years," that means everyone, regardless of his or her competency.

The good news is that those committed to superior work and lifestyle are always employable. They have surpassed being good workers or dependable employees. They have set their own standards high and they readily move into new positions.

Let's visit the executive conference room of one company and show how downsizing works.

After the CEO has gotten everyone's attention, he says, "Ladies and gentlemen, you are the leaders of this organization. I am going to rely on you to help turn this ship around. We have drifted from our purpose of being a top, profit-making company, and we've lost a great deal of money over the past four years. As a result, bankers and shareholders have given me no choice. If we do not turn this ship around, we will run aground. The situation is that serious."

To make certain everyone grasps the gravity of the situation—as if everyone doesn't already know—he says, "I have already asked a number of your peers for their resignations. You are in this room right now because you have been chosen to lead us through these tough times to help us save the ship."

I assure you that no one is smiling at that point. I know, because I've made similar speeches, although I admit that I wasn't as succinct or as focused. I've never found it easy to fire a large number of people and the words never come easy.

"Here is what we must do." The CEO clears his throat as his gaze surveys everyone in the room. "Based on current and projected sales for the remainder of this year, we have established a head count that we must reduce the company down to. Each of you will be forced to reduce your staff by 20 percent, and that means we begin to downsize everyone who has been with the corporation less than a year. If we do not reach that percentage, we'll go back as far as two years or three.

"I am also asking you to be certain that the level of

productivity does not drop with this drastic downsizing. This change will demand more work from each of us, but this is what we must do if we are going to turn this ship around. All of us must be committed to the best we have to offer."

Usually when I share this story with groups of employees in a seminar format, no one acts surprised. In fact, the first few times it amazed me to realize how many were familiar with the scenario. Some of them could even have made the speech for me.

At least a third of them usually nodded, because they knew exactly where I was heading.

"But what would it be like if the CEO changed his speech?" I usually ask. "What would happen if he didn't talk about such things as cutting 20 percent or getting rid of those who had been hired within the last year? How could he turn the company around without resorting to such measures?

"I'll show you how—and this illustrates the principle of Unconditional Excellence.

"The company is facing hard economic times, as all organizations do somewhere in their history. At some point, even the best companies face downsizing." I'd probably start there as my introduction. "I want each of you to go through your employee lists. As you do, choose the ones who are the least capable of making it through these tough times. Those are the ones we need to dismiss.

"Choose the ones with the worst attitudes and the least to offer. Choose the ones who don't work well with others in teams, who consistently miss deadlines, and who cannot communicate well. Those are the ones we need to downsize.

"Pick those who are not able to take initiative or solve problems. Find the ones who do not take personal responsibility for their actions or who will not attempt to lead others. Give me those who respond only when you reward them for producing beyond normal expectations. We will get rid of them.

"Give me a list of the whiners and complainers, those who are consistently late or absent and especially those who bring out the worst in others. They will be among the first to go."

This isn't a hypothetical speech; this is a speech I've had to give twice. Here's how I end it: "We will downsize those individuals, because they are the ones who will hinder us from building this company back to achieve top success and profitability. They are the people who prevent *us* from being unconditionally outstanding as a company."

When I talk that way, I want to be certain everyone understands this isn't a matter of seniority or some kind of squatter's rights. This is business. One of our objectives is to remain a profit-making company.

It's interesting that as soon as I mention people such as the complainers and the lazy, every executive knows exactly the people I refer to. They do stand out—for the wrong reasons.

In that little speech, I go on to draw a sharp distinction between valuable, employable workers and those who barely do their work (or don't do it) and hinder the productivity of others.

Again, I want to point out that even in a company committed to achieving the best and highest goals, economic conditions may mean some of those outstanding employees still end up losing their jobs in downsizing because we have to cut so

deep into the layoff numbers. However, they should represent a
very small number.

Most companies want to hire and keep the best employees,
not the worst. Unfortunately, some exceptional employees do get
caught in downsizing when organizations need to cut a large
number of people.

This makes my point even more significant: In uncertain
economic times, there is no greater job security than being an
employee of the highest caliber and personal character.
Lifetime employment is an outdated concept and employability
is our responsibility. We remain desirable and employable
because of our character and our performance.

By accepting the challenge laid out in this book, not only
can you learn to apply practical principles in your career, you
will be applying godly values in the process. It is a win-win-win
situation. You win, your employer wins, and God is honored.

Beginning of Excellence

After a speech I made to his company on "Unconditional
Leadership Excellence," a young executive asked me, "When did
you first begin applying these guiding principles?"

"I wasn't born with these ideas packed inside my head," I
replied. With a little trepidation, I went on, "It happened during
what would be the last phases of the Vietnam War, and it began
with a question asked me by 'Feet' Motley."

Momentarily, I closed my eyes. Although this happened in

1971, the memory is still fresh in my mind. As a young reservist, barely twenty years old, I was in basic training with nineteen other reservists, all of whom would be returning to the safety of our normal lives. Training alongside us were 205 others, draftees and enlistees, who were being prepared for war.

Because most of us in that reserve unit had some college as well as ROTC training, we became the acting platoon and squad leaders for the company. For the first few weeks, I took my leadership role lightly, concerned with making it through those hellish weeks, and I didn't give much thought to those in my platoon—all younger than me by a year or two. The other reservists acted about the same way I did.

Our lead drill instructor, Sergeant Taylor, must have sensed our lack of concern and lack of leadership commitment, because he called several of us into his room one evening.

He was a man of few, but very select, words. "Gentlemen, I asked you here because I need your help. Most of you will complete this training, and after a few months you will be discharged from active duty, return home to your girlfriends, jobs, and everyday lives. The rest of these young men have been given to me for one specific purpose. My job is to get them ready for war. Most likely, within a few months, all of them will end up in Vietnam. Many of them will be injured. Some will be killed."

He waited for those words to sink in and all of us became aware of the prolonged silence.

His words did get deep inside my head, and I felt ashamed at my cavalier attitude toward those young men.

"I intend to train them, lead them, and prepare them to live, not to die. I ask that you understand the responsibility each of you has to these men and to yourself. You have a chance to leave a legacy here. Can I trust you to do that along with me? Can I trust you to lead by giving your very best, not for what you will gain, but for what you will give? And for whom you might save?"

A legacy. Something about that word surged through my brain and wouldn't let go. I could leave a legacy. By definition, legacy can mean an inheritance or something we hand down to those who come after us.

"I can leave a legacy for these men," I said to myself after the briefing. "What a challenge!"

The seeds of my commitment to a leadership legacy had been planted that evening.

Later that same evening Feet Motley came into my room. He was a scared, seventeen-year-old enlistee from East St. Louis. He was black; I was white. He was poor; I was middle class. He was scared, and I was his leader.

"I don't think I can do this. I just can't." He was close to tears. "I just want to go home. I thought I wanted to be in the army, I really did, but I just want to go home now." The tears seeped from his eyes and he made no attempt to hide them. "What should I do?"

I sat silently, staring at him. His eager face forced me to admit that Sergeant Taylor had been right and I had focused more on myself than I had on these kids. I had absolutely no idea what to say. My joke of two days earlier suddenly haunted me. I had laughingly told him that, because his feet were so big, he would probably be blown up by a land mine in Vietnam.

Everybody laughed at the time. Even Feet laughed.

Now I felt ashamed for having made the joke.

"Why did you join up?" I asked. "You might have gotten a low draft number. Maybe you could have avoided this whole war. You're only seventeen, so you weren't eligible for the draft yet. Why did you do it?"

He looked up at me. Tears still streaked his face. "Because I'm supposed to do my best. I'm supposed to give it all I got and not hold back. I thought this was my chance to get out of East St. Louis, to make my mamma proud. I talked to my pastor about it and he told me God had great plans for me if I trusted him. I do trust God."

"I know you do, Bruce." It was the first time I had ever used his given name. "I know you do." We sat for a long while before either of us spoke again. He dropped his head; I couldn't turn my gaze away from his fear-filled face.

"What did you expect when you joined the Army?" I asked.

"A chance," he replied quickly. "Just a chance. I wanted to make a difference. Where I come from, it's hard to make a difference. I wanted to give God my best and—and help other people. That seemed like the best way and that's what I've been trying to do."

His words stunned me. That poor, uneducated kid said something that would stay with me forever. "I wanted to make a difference." The seeds had been planted that morning by my sergeant. Now they came to fruition through the words of the private.

This became my first glimpse of what would become my passion and goal in life, not only to give myself unstintingly to others, but also to teach them to do the same. This started because one man—a child really—had committed himself unreservedly to God. Would God be pleased with that commitment? Was it an acceptable sacrifice? Could Bruce "Feet" Motley really make a difference? That night, as I observed the intensity on his face, despite his being scared, I believed that he could.

In a strange way, in that moment, I knew that I also could make a difference in the world.

To this day I will never forget that the "call" from Sergeant Taylor to be a leader who built a legacy challenged my thinking. The words of the young man gave me a sharp focus.

Throughout the ten weeks we were together, Bruce taught me something valuable about God. He taught me to give my best. Even more, he taught me that *how* we do things is as important as *what* we do.

Bruce and I had many other late night talks and he did make it through training. His love of life and his quick-and-easy smile, along with his desire to excel, was not only evident, but it grew stronger. I'm not sure he ever totally lost his fear, but he never wavered again in his commitment to make a difference.

I like to believe that in the final weeks of training, I taught Bruce enough to survive. Later, I learned that he had been shipped to Vietnam. That's the last I ever heard about him. I hope he came home. I'll bet he made a difference and that his mama in East St. Louis was proud of him.

A Business Legacy

How does this account apply to the business world? What possible relevance can this incident have to what we do in our day-to-day jobs? Obviously, we aren't involved in life-and-death situations.

This isn't war.

Or maybe it *is* war—war of a different kind.

Each of us is involved in an epic struggle. We can fight it in a variety of ways. It's a battle to live with integrity or to be a person of honor. As a Christian, I think of it as spiritual warfare. Every day I encounter people who want to take ethical shortcuts, try questionable but barely legal maneuvers, or blatantly lie to customers or employees. The struggle to fight off such commonly accepted methods is, to me, spiritual warfare. It is a struggle for us to choose between what is right and what is wrong, between good and evil.

Sometimes the struggle is between what's expedient and what's right, or between the good and best. Regardless, it's always a struggle for us to stand firm, to hold strongly to what we believe, and to insist on the standard of Unconditional Excellence in ourselves, regardless of how others around us behave.

Our battlefield isn't as clearly defined as in Vietnam, but we still wage war against those in our offices, manufacturing plants, and construction sites who oppose our giving our best or who try to tempt us to settle for less than the best.

In the Battles

How are Christians doing in the battle?

Rather poorly, if we ask people who work with us, sell to us, or buy from us. Some Christians are angry and self-righteous. Some shirk responsibility. There are always those who are more preoccupied with eternal matters than with the temporal tasks that make up the world of business.

For instance, one day when I was doing a survey at one company, I asked one department manager about another.

"The biggest problem I have with Sid," Marty said, "is that he is more interested in talking about Jesus Christ than he is in acting like him."

Marty himself exhibited little interest in spiritual matters, but he was an invaluable employee because his bosses knew they could rely on him to perform his work with zeal and quality. While Marty seemed to know little about the Bible, he was able to grasp the disconnect between what Sid said and what Sid did.

At the other end of the spectrum was this comment from Tom about Ken, who was the owner of the company he worked for. "It really came as a shock to me when I found out that an affair was going on in the office between the COO [Chief Operating Officer] and the woman in charge of information systems. I knew they had to work closely together, but I always assumed the COO, who was a professing Christian, was above that sort of behavior.

"Even more disturbing to me is that, for at least four

months, Ken knew about that affair, and he didn't fix the problem." Tom shook his head in disbelief. "He's the owner who constantly reminds us that this is Christ's company, and that we are stewards of it, and we need to exhibit the most godly behavior."

His eyes narrowed and he said, "I'll tell you something else. Because Ken let this go on, he's become a real joke out in the plant. Those out there on the line have no respect for Ken and they despise the COO. It makes me want to hide my faith rather than share it openly."

Although I have changed the names, these two illustrations are true; I wish they were fiction.

Think for a moment of a situation in your career when a believer blew it. What impact did it have on the rest of the people in the organization? Too often we're quick to defend the errors and mediocrity of our work and that of our fellow believers. To help those in trouble is honorable; to condone bad behavior of any kind is wrong.

Most of us have seen the bumper sticker that reads, "Christians aren't perfect, just forgiven." The fallacy in that statement is that we grab on to the concept of forgiveness—which is absolutely true—but forget that's only part of it. My concept of forgiveness follows the words said to one woman, "Go, and sin no more."

As those who choose to live by the highest and most ethical standards, we can't just talk about forgiveness as if that takes away the burden of achieving the best we're capable of.

Being Examples

To witness means to model a lifestyle, to be an example for others to see, and to reflect what we have seen and experienced. Too often we have turned being a witness into a religious exercise.

Isn't it time for us to ask ourselves serious questions? Here are a few of them:

- What do my employees, employers, and coworkers see (or witness) about the way I work?
- What kind of example am I of excellence?
- What will customers see and understand from the actions and interactions they have with the employees in our company?
- Will they see my unqualified commitment at work?
- Will they see only acceptable behavior?
- Will they speak of unacceptable behavior?
- What should my boss expect from me?
- What kind of testimony am I being to them of my way of life?

Giving ourselves to our tasks and settling for nothing less than the best needs to be a way of life for every person in the workplace today. We need to make it a standard of achievement if we are to live meaningfully and leave a legacy of fulfilled lives. Unconditional Excellence is for everyone, not just the initiated.

The principles that will make a difference, while they are all biblically based, are not exclusive to one group or another.

Although I believe the Christian in the marketplace has a higher calling to live according to these principles, I will provide many clear illustrations of people who work accordingly without a spiritual call to do so. It rains on both the believers and the nonbelievers.

Finally, I want to emphasize that this principle works. Even though I share these insights from my experience as a Christian, it doesn't matter, really, whether you're Christian, Buddhist, Jewish, or whether you have no religion. Unconditional Excellence works because these are eternal, immutable truths.

chapter two

A Covenant of Excellence

After I coined the phrase *covenantal relationships* in the business world, a number of people I respected advised me the term would never fly.

Typical of their comments:

- "Covenant is an old-fashioned word. People don't understand it."
- "The marketplace lives by contracts. Covenants are part of contracts, so why do you believe covenantal relationships are more important or valid than contractual relationships?"
- "We don't do business by a handshake anymore. If we did, a lot of law schools would shut down."
- "Covenantal thinking is for the religious world, not the business world."

With each objection, I became more convinced of the need for a change in the way we relate in the business world, especially for people who should have an eternal perspective. Since

1996, I have made the term *covenantal principles* part of my vocabulary when I work with companies and individuals. I can attest to its effectiveness and the impact it has had.

The difficulty we have with the concept of covenant arises from our fear that if we go the extra mile, people will take advantage of us. That's possible and even probable, if we assume covenants are that limiting. They are not. *Covenants are a foundational principle of Unconditional Excellence.*

Let's start with a definition, because the principle of the covenant plays a vital role in our becoming Unconditionally Excellent. *A covenantal relationship means always doing what is in the best interest of the other, in pursuit of the vision, mission, or objectives of the company.*

For us to be covenantal in the workplace implies that we labor toward fulfilling the highest standards. We refuse to let the work of our hands destroy the example of our lives. This begins with leaders who commit themselves to these principles by modeling and teaching them as they lead with excellence. I also want to make it clear that Unconditional Excellence isn't just for leaders. This is for everyone who collects a paycheck. No matter what our job or responsibility, we can commit ourselves to this higher calling—and *it is* a higher calling.

The advent of the professional church leader becomes a phenomenon well after Christ. He didn't surround himself with the professional clergy. His first followers were among the common people—fishermen and tax collectors. I don't oppose professional religious leaders, but I think we make a mistake to label their career choice as a "higher calling." By implication this means that the rest of us have a "lower calling." Such labeling has led to compartmentalized lives, a splintered faith, and a religion lacking the power that Jesus Christ came to earth to give us.

The appeal to Unconditional Excellence means we strive for results that are beyond what any company asks or demands of its employees. Doesn't that imply we have a higher calling than those who do only what is required of them? I see this not as a choice but as part of our commitment to excellence in service to God. Jesus once said that we can't serve two masters. When we aim for excellence in the workplace, our highest service to God manifests itself by the quality of our work and relationships. Unconditional Excellence is an unstated but integral part of *covenantal* relationship—the code of life God calls us to live by.

It is possible to be part of a successful, profitable company without being covenantal; it is impossible to live with Unconditional Excellence without experiencing the incredible power of a covenant relationship. The apostle Paul modeled this concept by doing what was in the best interest of others, regardless of the personal cost.

Covenants and Contracts

I like to contrast covenants with contracts or agreements. Contracts create and limit expectations and outcome. That is, they lay out the consequences of not living up to the stipulations of the agreement. Although such words may sound good, they also restrict the conditions and the results.

By contrast, covenants release employees to exceed the legal or expected requirements. Covenants ask, "What is possible? What *more* can I do?" Contracts state what is permissible and lay down limitations. Covenantal agreements enable people to ask "What if . . . ?" and unleash collective brilliance and individual excellence. Covenants with fellow employees take us to a standard beyond what most employers expect. That's the problem. We have been able to lower our standards to a worldly level, missing the power of godly principles.

Obviously, it's easier to live by a lower standard, yet we are not called to lower our standards. Our purpose is to raise them.

We covenant within our organization when we set the highest standards of opportunity, excellence, and responsibility. For the most part, that is the heart of a covenant: making the most of our potential, whether with customers, coworkers, or employees. Covenants are practical expressions of our maximum potential; that also makes them practical applications of our maximum effort. We won't achieve maximum potential without maximum effort from every employee within the organization.

If companies operate by the highest principles, they achieve financial profitability, but profit is the byproduct of a much greater result. When we are covenantal, we don't ignore the important aspects that make business profitable. Because they're not *intrinsic* values, however, these important aspects don't produce eternal value. In fact, making money is the easy part of operating a company. If all we had to do was to make a company profitable or cash positive, our job would be easily defined and simpler. We would use people to accomplish things that create a profit. When we add the covenant component, we create a complexity that involves time, individual and collective desires, and a tension between valuing people while we create value.

The tension between valuing people and creating value causes most of us to avoid covenantal relationships. When we do find the balance between the two—making it a creative rather than a destructive tension—we unleash others' true potential. How could we possibly value people more than by helping them achieve maximum potential?

What's difficult—and this is what takes us into covenantal responsibility—is that we take those commonly accepted goals of making a profit and increasing the shareholder's value, and we turn them upside down. What many use within other organizations to measure success and top-priority achievements, we accept as an *outcome* of living by covenantal commitment to unqualified excellence.

We create intrinsic value by bringing out the very best in ourselves and in those who work with us. Not only do we value our coworkers, we value them for the right reasons—and they know it. They don't see themselves as steps for us to climb on our upward move. By our attitude, we symbolically join hands so that all of us move forward together. We set high-level expectations for our performance and our relationships. Amazingly, others measure up to those standards.

We strive to be long-term winners. Our organization doesn't have to be number one in the marketplace, but by constantly learning how to improve everything we do, we do whatever we can to enable our company always to be in the lead. We survive changes in our particular field, our leadership and organizations are secure, and everyone knows they can depend on us. External and internal changes in business don't overwhelm, threaten, or disrupt us. We're prepared for whatever comes; we're always ready to adapt, to transform ourselves, and even to reinvent ourselves when necessary.

At a recent seminar, I asked, "What would a covenantal relationship look like with one of your customers?"

"We would get the product to them instantly, guaranteed to work, and then we would pick up the buyers' keys and wash their cars," said Mindy, manager of a customer service department. Everybody laughed.

Obviously, Mindy has had some bad experiences with demanding customers.

Read the serious part of her answer again: "We would get the product to them instantly, guaranteed to work." Although she was correct in what she said, Mindy saw only a one-sided responsibility. There are two sides. The counterbalance to "doing what is in the best interest" lies in fulfillment of the vision, mission, or objectives of the company. (I'll explain this further.)

Clarity of Vision

What happens if the company, the department, or the office I work in doesn't have a clear vision, mission, or purpose? As much money as companies have spent on creating company mission statements, I am amazed how little clarity they have in terms of mission and purpose.

Several years ago I conducted a competitive immersion project for a nationally recognized and highly respected client. The CEO was concerned that they had become stodgy and complacent. He worried that technology would allow competitors to leapfrog them in the marketplace. My job was to shake them out of the mentality that said, "We are the industry standard and cannot be usurped."

My first challenge was to see if the executive team was aligned to the vision of the company. Their mission statement, by the way, was clearly visible on a plaque in the lobby of their home office in Providence, Rhode Island. I learned later that they had paid a consultant nearly $100,000 for help in developing that statement.

During our first group session in the executive conference room, I asked them to tell me their mission statement. Before they entered the room I had removed a smaller plaque from the wall, which they could have read. I also asked them not to open their binders or wallets, since the statement had been printed on plastic cards for easy referral.

Several blank faces stared back at me.

Not one of the seven people in that room could recite it. The CEO came closest, capturing the essence of the words, yet even he missed some of the most important parts.

"Think of me as a customer," I said. "What does your statement mean to me? What should I experience from your people if you are living your vision and accomplishing your mission statement?"

More blank stares before they looked at each other. Then they began to see my point. If the leaders didn't know how their grand statement applied to the day-to-day interactions they had with customers, suppliers, and each other, how could they assume direct-report employees applied it? To most employees, their vision, no matter how eloquent, remained a plaque on the wall or a statement on the back of a business card. No one had a clear understanding of purpose or mission.

This experience, unfortunately, is the norm, not the exception.

Vision is not some far-off-in-the-distance destination. Vision is what people experience every day as we "live the vision." Mission is not some pithy statement on a plaque in the lobby. It is the reason we are in business. Vision and mission define the purpose of an organization.

What We Do First

Before we can attempt a covenant relationship, we must first determine what it means to fulfill the vision, mission, or purpose of the organization. Our purpose can be defined either in collective corporate terms or in individual areas of purpose, but it must be identified for every individual. Then we have the counterbalance to be "in the best interest of the other."

A covenantal relationship means always doing what is in the best interest of the other, in pursuit of the vision, mission, or objectives of the company.

Here's another example. When I was CEO of the Fellowship of Companies for Christ, we developed a three-month process on just these issues. Every month we came together for three days at the Masters Institute. It was the first time I introduced the principles I now refer to as Unconditional Excellence.

As soon as I finished, the next speaker—one of nine CEOs at the meeting—said, "This will never work. My employees would just take advantage of me if I told them I wanted to begin living by covenantal relationships."

I explained the idea of covenant again, but he was ready with a question.

"What happens when you have to fire an employee and she comes back and accuses you of not being covenantal? It certainly isn't in her best interest to get fired." Everybody chuckled.

"Why would you want to fire an employee?" I asked, pointing to one business owner.

"I assume she or he did something that would warrant termination."

"Of course. That's the only reason you would do it," another replied.

"Give me an example of a situation that caused you to terminate an employee recently," I asked the group. "Let's not deal in hypothetical situations, but with our real-world experiences."

"One of our drivers got his third speeding ticket within the last six months," volunteered Chuck. "The company rules are clear. Three moving violations within a twelve-month period and you're terminated. Our insurance carrier wouldn't insure us if we didn't have policies like that.

"When his supervisor let him go, he understood the rules and accepted it. If we had this covenantal relationship principle as part of the expectation, I'm not sure it would have been that easy or that clear."

"Is safety part of your mission and one of the key components of how you evaluate your drivers?" I asked.

"Definitely."

"There is the counterbalance for you. Was it in the driver's best interest and that of the entire company to maintain a good safety record?"

He nodded.

"You have defined it clearly in this instance. I don't think you have made it more difficult," I said. "After you fired your driver, I imagine the rest of your drivers understood the seriousness of this safety policy." I paused because this was an important point for them to agree on. "Whether you used the word *covenant* isn't the point. You hired the driver, and he knew what was expected of him. Therefore, there was a mutual responsibility for both parties."

Then they understood.

Hundreds of companies, with thousands of employees, are experiencing the benefits of Unconditional Excellence based on that foundational principle. In business, it may be the most significant biblical principle we ever apply, and Jesus modeled it better than anyone else. He always did what was in the best interest of others, on behalf of a much greater purpose. Can we—should we—do less?

Jim Dismore is the CEO of Ultimate Support Systems (USS), a growing manufacturer of musical instrument stands and equipment. I worked with the executive leadership team at

USS when they began to apply and expand on my principles.

Two remarkable things struck me about USS:

First was the alignment throughout the company with the principle of Unconditional Excellence. They didn't use those words, but leaders treated each other covenantally and employees gave the same kind of treatment to each other and to customers and suppliers. The quality and value of their products made their good working relationships evident, but even more important, the relationships they established made their commitment to excellence obvious.

I watched the entire leadership team grapple with the concept that the "quality of our work" would be the true measurement of their commitment to excellence. The excellence of their work showed their values. What also struck me was the extent to which the leaders challenged each other to value the people, which in turn created great respect within the company.

It was a refreshing experience to frequently hear leaders say, "We value people."

Too often and in too many other organizations, as soon as financial value is threatened, leaders squeeze the hardest those whom they supposedly value. At USS, people are respected and esteemed during the good times. They are just as valued during the down times.

The second remarkable aspect of USS is their approach to what many call ministry. They encourage and empower employees to use their time and the company's resources to influence Fort Collins, Colorado. Regardless of religious affiliation, employees share in the good works that USS sponsor. Jim

Dismore leads and his people follow his example. Theirs is a bright light, made brighter by their sense of unity and commitment to a common goal.

Purpose of Unconditional Excellence

I decided to write this book to help Christians in the marketplace live relevant lives and to become credible messengers. Pastors preach sermons and write books about turning to Jesus Christ and living faithful lives. They do a good job, and they reach out to people. Then comes the problem. For most of us, there's a huge disconnect on Monday morning. As soon as the garage door goes up and we back out our cars, we're moving into the tyranny of the marketplace.

It is just that—the fast pace is demanding, vicious, scary, and unforgiving if we don't measure up. If we're not on guard, our jobs suck all the life out of us. As we start driving toward our places of work, we forget what we heard at church. The wonderful advice of pastors and Sunday school teachers seems irrelevant on Monday morning when your boss is expecting the impossible, the customers are overly demanding, and someone broke your favorite coffee mug over the weekend.

So what can we do?

I want to take biblical truth and then provide tools for people in the workplace. They can then apply these practical maxims and live their faith at work. They don't have to put their Christian beliefs on hold for six days or close it off until they drive out of the work parking lot on Friday.

Competency, Character, and Caring

In the 1960s, the Communist Party in Italy received enough
votes in the election to form a government. They chose not to.
Why? One of their leaders stated that until then, the nation had
judged the party based on its intentions. If it actually formed a
government, the party would be judged by its actions.

As a motive, the commitment to Unconditional Excellence
is well intentioned. But if we don't develop the skills necessary
to live up to that commitment, our actions will prove less than
our best. Our great intentions then become just another plaque
to hang on the wall.

I present three developmental approaches in this book:

1. Growing our competence.
2. Growing our character.
3. Challenging our capacity for caring.

All three are critical aspects to functioning at our total best.
Yet, as I have been through the marketplace, I see that most
people select one approach and tend to exclude the other two.

Applied Skill Development

In the workplace we need two specific skill sets—technical
or functional skills, and what we call "applied" skills. As we
move up into leadership positions within companies, the need
for our technical skills decreases as the need for our applied
skills increases. Yet too many companies spend little to no time

or money developing the skills that make the greatest difference in the profitability and long-term productivity of the company—the applied skills.

Applied skills are today's most important workforce. This is true whether we're CEOs or shipping clerks. The application and the scope of the skill changes by position, but the skill is still the same.

Character Development

This is undergoing a recent surge in popularity. Employers are realizing that character matters when it comes to creating long-term value in companies. It is essential to esteem people while we create financial values.

Having led hundreds of employees through seminars on Unconditional Excellence, I am always delighted when we complete the character section of the program. Inevitably a number of individuals will come up to me or write on the evaluations that they never realized the importance character played and the way they can develop character.

Challenging Our Capacity for Caring

Caring is actually a byproduct of the entire process of achieving Unconditional Excellence. "Caring" has become a wimpy, overused, and almost meaningless word. Politicians have virtually destroyed its meaning: They always seem to "care" deeply during an election, yet many of their votes while in office indicate a greater concern and caring for re-election than for our well-being. When others hear about our troubles or hardships, they flippantly say, "I care." Perhaps they do, but the test is the actions that follow such words. A daily advice columnist often closes her comments with the words, "I care." Maybe she does, but it's hard for me to believe those words have any real meaning for her anonymous reader.

Let's not throw out the word, though. Caring in the business world is an important part of Unconditional Excellence. I want to show that caring isn't just a fad term or jargon. Caring, when properly understood, is extremely practical.

The Source of Excellence

One of my greatest concerns as we learn the power and the purpose of Unconditional Excellence is that we live the example of the qualities we stress. There is much we can do to apply those life-changing principles, and the real power comes from a different source. The title of this book should have suggested that God has a hand in each of our lives. We who follow the tenets of the Bible also realize that Jesus Christ is the ultimate model and the source for all our excellence.

My continuing discovery of my own role in living out that excellence is what keeps me enthusiastic. It's what makes me alive and alert when I get up out of bed and take on another business day.

Aside from the subjective value, here's what I really like about these principles: *They work,* regardless of whether we subscribe to the same faith or have no faith. These principles of God function, and they thrive with astonishing success in the business world. Maybe we have merely forgotten some of the most basic and powerful biblical concepts that our grandparents and their grandparents took for granted. I hope one day these principles will be assumed and accepted by everyone. If that happens, then they will have become the standard we try to achieve.

Integrating the Secular and the Sacred

Another easy mistake is to think that Unconditional Excellence is something we do that is separated from our work. If that were the case, we wouldn't have enough time to be excellent: Time is the currency of the moment in the workplace. Who doesn't already have more work than he or she needs or wants? Who isn't overloaded? How could we add excellence as one more thing to our hectic schedules?

To become Unconditionally Excellent we don't need to add anything. Instead, we need to learn to apply those principles while we do our daily tasks. Everything we do that moves us toward that goal moves us away from the tyranny of the urgent and into living more fully in the present.

In the years that I've been teaching these concepts, many people comment, write, phone, fax, and e-mail me about how dramatically this has influenced their personal effectiveness, job performance, and productivity. They also add that by being covenantal it's becoming easier to function than it was without such understandings.

But they all had to start. They all had to move from good intentions into action.

chapter three

Personal Destiny and Purpose

In the 1990s a small group of us, all business people from different companies, used to meet for breakfast every other week for what I called "discipling in leadership"—to help others become more effective leaders in the workplace. Among the group were Randy Macall, a midlevel manager with AT&T, and Kevan Sears, a national sales manager for a local company. A third member, Nick Richardson, was an excellent computer systems specialist who loved evangelism and could talk to anyone about his faith in Jesus Christ.

We were intent on helping each other develop our full potential in every aspect of our lives: at work, in our families, and through our churches.

One morning as I watched Nick head toward our table, everything about him shouted that he was discouraged, even the way he walked. His shoulders sagged, and his usual smile didn't appear when he shook hands.

We encouraged him to tell us what was going on. We were aware that two months earlier he had gotten a new boss, named Barbara, who became the regional manager of Nick's group.

Nick had been telling us, in the weeks that followed her promotion, that Barbara was extremely task-oriented and not very relationship-oriented. "I'm going nowhere fast with her," he had said several times.

That particular morning, his face signaled a serious problem. He had barely seated himself before he blurted out, "She put me on probation."

We knew who *she* referred to.

"I'm good at what I do, and I've never been on probation in my life."

Wisely, we let Nick talk, and he soon let us know that he felt powerless, believing that she would use the probation as the first step toward firing or easing him out of his job. If he lost his job, he could find another one, but he had never been terminated. The probation status humiliated him. "She's the cause of it all," he said, the anger mounting in his voice. "Until she became my boss, I'd always gotten good reviews and even praise for my work."

During several breakfast meetings, Nick had mentioned that he wanted to get out of the corporate world because he just didn't enjoy the work any more. For the past two years, Nick had told us repeatedly that he yearned for the opportunity to work full-time for God. "I'm tired of this rat race. I'm tired of doing all of this stuff in the company. I want to do God's work. This pressure is on, and maybe this is God's hand allowing me to go into the ministry."

"You said you wanted a clear sign from God about your career," I said jokingly. "Sounds like an answer to prayer."

He didn't think my remark was funny.

"If you leave," Randy asked, "then what will you do?"

"I don't know, but if God is orchestrating this, God will provide."

"Have you also considered that God may *not* be orchestrating this?" Kevan asked.

Nick nodded and again stressed his burning desire to serve God. "I want to serve God so badly. Maybe this *is* God's message for me."

"Something's wrong here," I said after several minutes. "I don't think this is right. I can't believe God would lead you into full-time ministry because of a disastrous failure in your job." I wasn't fully clear yet about what I wanted to say, so I asked Nick if we could meet privately and talk in more depth on the topic. He agreed.

After Kevan and Randy left, I said, "I've listened to you complain about your work ever since Barbara became your supervisor. Two things occur to me. First, I think the major issue is you can't submit to the authority of a woman. You always talk about working for God somewhere, and I can't imagine a better place to start than right—"

"Well, I—I—" he stammered, and I knew he hadn't considered that possibility.

"Have you ever submitted to the authority of a woman at work?" I knew Nick's religious background and this ran contrary to many of the things he had been taught. "This is hard for you, isn't it?"

He nodded slowly. "Maybe there is some truth to that. I

have a hard time submitting to her authority."

He's not alone in this area either. I find it amazing how difficult it is for some religious males to submit to females. Women leaders have shared that it's not just men: Other women have a difficult time submitting to them, simply because they're the same gender. Just as unfortunate, many employees also have difficulty submitting to leaders of different ethnic backgrounds.

I want to make this principle clear: The core of Unconditional Excellence is that we submit to and support those who have authority over us. We do that regardless of their gender, ethnicity, or educational background. If we can't jump over this hurdle, we lower the standard to a level below mediocrity. Much of our potential is wasted on fighting those in authority rather than supporting them. Nick's story is just one such instance.

"I want to tell you the second thing that occurs to me," I told him. "Barbara criticizes you the most about the amount of time that you spend in relationships, right? As you build those relationships, you talk about your faith. You tell people about God and their spiritual need."

"That's right, and that's because it's my gift to spread the word. My former supervisor was a believer. He understood and—"

I held up my hand. "You had freedom to do that with your previous supervisor, but not now. This woman is raining on your evangelistic parade. Isn't she?"

At first he said nothing, then he nodded again slowly and said, "Yes."

"What is the reason that she gives for her attitude? Is it

that she's under pressure? You told me the whole region is under enormous pressure. Does she need you to work more and talk less? Do you really think Barbara is against your sharing what you believe? Or is she more concerned about your sharing the workload?"

To his credit, Nick made no attempt to defend himself.

"Think about what you would need if you were the supervisor for your region. Barbara needs your best efforts and your skills right now far more than you realize. Instead of helping her, you're negative, you have a lousy attitude, and you've become a sullen worker. That's not the example of Christ's excellence you talk about, is it?"

He dropped his gaze, and I knew he was listening carefully.

"She needs you to focus on the things that are important to the company. Instead, you focus on the things that are important to Nick. If I were in Barbara's position, I'd probably have fired your butt."

Those words startled him, but once the shock had subsided he said, "You're right."

"When she's putting on pressure to get more work from you, you're fighting her. That means you're wasting more company time working against her. You're angry and hostile." (Several times at our meetings Nick had vented about Barbara to the point that it became obvious no manager could be as bad as he purported her to be.)

I knew this wasn't easy for him to hear, but he kept listening.

"You've become angry and mean-spirited. She's your boss

and you're hostile to her. As a Christian, knowing you represent the most excellent way, have you ever gone to her and asked, 'How do I serve you?'"

"No, of course not."

"You're too busy trying to do God's work in your office! In reality, the best way to do that would be to model what Jesus modeled."

I stopped and let him talk. I wanted to know how much of my message he had absorbed. I admired him for being able to hear what I said and to accept the truth.

"What should I do?" he finally asked.

"You said you hadn't gone to her and asked, 'How can I serve you?' So will you do that? As a favor to me—even if you're not convinced that's the best thing to do—will you ask that question? If she says, 'You can serve me by leaving,' maybe God is guiding to get you out of there. But think about this: *Is it possible that God wants you to stay and work in harmony with her?* You don't know the answer to that question yet, do you?"

"No, I really don't."

"Even if she asks you to leave, now or in two months or six, will you do one more thing? Until she asks for your resignation, will you commit yourself to being excellent at what you do in your job? As long as you are there, will you become part of *her* team? Will you help *her* succeed? Will you try to understand the pressure she's under and find ways to add value to her life by adding value to your work? Be excellent, Nick. That's all you need to do."

"Yes, yes, I can do that."

"Barbara needs your commitment now. You can be the support she needs, and when you get behind her, you're not just doing it for her; you're also doing it as service to Jesus Christ. Maybe God wants her to be able to see your faith through your commitment to serve rather than through the words you speak. In fact, supporting her may be your best evangelistic message."

I have to admire Nick for doing exactly as I asked. He talked to his supervisor and phoned me later that day.

"It was really quite amazing. First, my words absolutely shocked her. I realized that she probably never expected to hear me talk that way. She explained about the pressures she's under. She said she wanted to work with me, but didn't know how to talk to me." He laughed ruefully, "She said that ever since she had taken over she felt my hostility toward her." He paused and I could tell this affected him emotionally. "You know what makes me feel rotten? She said that she had heard many good things about me and had eagerly looked forward to working with me. My former boss told her I was one of the best leaders in the region, someone she could always count on. Alan, did I ever blow it. My bad attitude really came through."

He explained that Barbara accepted what she called his "religious convictions," but pointed out that they had work to do and were under heavier pressure than they had ever been. "I feel you haven't been supportive of me or the others in our department," she said. She explained she had put him on probation because he was more focused on what he wanted than what the company needed.

"I'm going to do everything I can to support you," Nick

promised. From that time on, he followed through on that promise.

To his amazement, within a couple of weeks Nick learned that Barbara was one of the best managers he had ever worked for. Barbara's behavior helped Nick overcome whatever reservations he had about working under a woman's supervision. She was also a great team leader, the kind that brings out the best in the group. Barbara felt the tyranny of the pressure of work just as much as he did, and he helped to support her when tensions increased.

About a month after Nick made his change, Barbara began to talk to him during their coffee breaks. She had a husband and a family and bemoaned the hours and effort it took for her to succeed. When she went home, she often didn't have the patience with her family that they deserved.

"She struggles just like I do," he said. "She's a real person."

They developed a warm working relationship. Barbara didn't give him the opportunity to quote Bible verses or talk often about his faith, but he realized that he was able to relate to her in a different way than he had expected. She listened to his suggestions and commended him several times for his diligence and faithfulness to the tasks.

Within a short time Nick not only had gotten off probation, but his excellence at his work took the pressure off. His leader learned to trust him and knew that he would be loyal to her and do his best to solve whatever problem existed.

Nick also became one of the important mentors in her

group. He excitedly told our breakfast group that whenever anybody had problems, Barbara called Nick and asked him to talk to that individual. "You're the best person I know to help him," she had said only the day before.

Eight months later, Barbara asked Nick to come to her office. "There's a job opening in the training division, and I've already recommended you for it, but I want to explain something to you. If you take this, I will hate to lose you. This isn't a promotion, but a lateral step. I know you hate to travel so it seems like a good fit for you. It will keep you here in Atlanta most of the time and you'll rarely have to travel."

Because he now knew her well, Nick didn't question the truthfulness of her words. More than ever, he realized how highly she valued him.

"As I said, I hate to lose you, but I think you'll be great at the job."

Because of her recommendation, Nick was interviewed and received the job. In fact, it became his dream job. He had finally found his niche in the business world. In his teaching position, he developed good, lasting relationships and touched many lives.

The best part of this true story is that the very person who sponsored him was the one who had been trying to get rid of him—and he had assumed it was because of his faith. When he changed his attitude and his tactics and began to strive to help her, he didn't hide his belief in Jesus Christ. Even more than before, he lived the life he spoke about.

I don't know where Nick is today because we've gone different ways, but I do know he didn't leave to become a professional minister. It was as if God said to him, "No, you're doing my ministry right where you are. You're going to be more effective for me in the marketplace than behind a pulpit."

Foundational Factors of Purpose

Every year *Forbes* magazine produces a list of the "100 Best Places to Work." They use more than twenty benefits and other criteria in determining their ratings. If we remove the benefits that apply only to very large corporations or to single-location employers (such as on-site day care) and the criteria not easily matched by the vast majority of employers, a fairly solid list remains.

At Corporate Development Institute (CDI), Inc., we have conducted what we call Employee Satisfaction Surveys that rate companies by how satisfied their employees are. We include many of the same benefits and criteria on the *Forbes* list. It's amazing how much broad agreement there is among employees about what they value from their careers.

There are six factors that can help employees and employers develop more satisfying and productive workplaces. All of these tie into finding personal motivation, which is what every employee wants from a job or career. And one of the greatest forces of motivators is personal destiny.

As simple as it sounds, after we review the list of factors, you will probably be able to recognize in your own current place of employment the gaps between what motivates you and what your employer provides. The good news is that Unconditional

Excellence helps you close those gaps.

The first three consistently head the list of employee satisfaction factors, but they're not the motivating factors. I refer to them as *foundation factors*. If employers increase the first three, productivity does not significantly increase. Although there may be a short-term blip in increased performance, within weeks the performance level drops to where it was before the increase in any of these three areas.

1. Pay

No one is surprised that the single most important factor leading to employee satisfaction is a good salary. Although no surprise, it's interesting that while it is clearly number one, it is really more of a maintenance factor than a motivating factor. More money by itself does not lead to satisfied, productive workers.

I'll bet there are a few CEOs who would love reading that so they could then say, "Aha, I knew it. I don't need to give raises. They don't work anyway." Sorry, boss, that isn't quite right either. Increased pay is not a motivator, and pay that is deemed unsatisfactory by employees is a demotivator. Give me more, and I'll perform better for a short period of time. Decrease my pay, and watch out! You'll have a disgruntled employee. I found this out the hard way, as illustrated shortly.

2. Benefits

This is no surprise either. Benefits are becoming increasingly important in two significant areas. The first is across-the-board health care. One of the most difficult problems many employees face is getting and keeping good insurance coverage. Health insurance is increasing in cost to employers and in importance to workers.

The second area is a tight labor market. During the dot-com craze, it was difficult finding key technology workers. One innovative company in Atlanta offered a unique benefit to make itself stand out from the crowd. They leased BMW Z3 sports cars for their technology staff. They received great press coverage, and they successfully recruited a number of employees. (Note to those of us who didn't get rich during the dot-com craze: I recently saw an ad in the *Atlanta Journal-Constitution* for a fleet sale of seventy-nine BMW Z3s.)

When the labor market tightens, benefit packages become one way we can attract and retain good employees; we know it is the second most important factor affecting career satisfaction.

3. Job Security

These first three sound rather obvious. It may be helpful to remind ourselves, however, that when companies make poor staffing decisions on the upside of an economic cycle, they pay a heavy price on the next downside.

In the early 1990s, I had the opportunity to lead companies through turnarounds. That was the toughest work I have ever done and either the least or most rewarding, depending on whether we saved the company.

At one company, the first thing I had to do was cut the staff by 20 percent. Production staff was relatively easy to trim because those employees were tied to plants and production lines, many of which had become idle. When it came to indirect workers and overhead employees, the job was tougher. With only two weeks to grasp the situation before we made the cuts, I had to decide on the leaders I would rely on to work with me to turn the company around. Then I made the first round of cuts.

I called a meeting of all my direct reports and laid out the game plan. I required each of them to make the necessary cuts in their area, such as eliminating quarterly bonuses, to get us to break even at a level of sales we thought we could sustain. That level, by the way, was approximately half of what the company was staffed for and about the same as they had achieved in the previous twelve-month period. Doesn't that make the need for a turnaround seem obvious?

I also announced that we had to take an across-the-board pay cut of 10 percent and that we would have to reduce some benefits. All of this worked fine on paper. The CFO assured me that the numbers would work.

What I didn't realize is that I had just hammered the people I needed to be the most productive because we were taking away two of the three most important factors that lead to job satisfaction—pay and benefits. The third, job security, had already been affected by the cutbacks.

The sales force underperformed. Engineering underper-formed. Manufacturing underperformed. Even my personal assistant seemed less productive than I had been promised she would be.

What happened? I should have expected exactly what I now know. Pay, benefits, and job security—the three factors employees say are most important for a satisfying career—become demotivating factors when taken away or reduced.

The good news is that there are three factors that truly motivate. Leaders can significantly affect the performance and productivity of their workers if they meet their needs in these three areas.

4. Meaningful Work

People want to know that what they do matters. I imagine an intensive care nurse at a children's hospital goes home every day knowing she made a difference and that her work matters. There are a few professions like that, where the work itself provides the meaning. For the majority of employees, however, we need to find meaning in our work in other ways. That is where great leadership distinguishes itself from the mediocre. Unconditionally Excellent leaders connect employees to a higher meaning and purpose, regardless of the nature of their work.

This is an old illustration, yet no matter how many times I hear it or tell it, I appreciate its meaning. A stranger sees a man digging a ditch. "What are you doing?" the stranger asks.

"Digging a ditch."

Next to him is another man, doing exactly the same thing. "And you, sir, what is it that you are doing?" the stranger asks.

"Digging a ditch," he replies. "When I am finished, my ditch and his ditch will create a trench."

Hmmm, there is more meaning in the work of the second man, thinks the stranger.

Finally he spots a third digger. "And you, are you digging a ditch, too?"

The third digger stares at the stranger before he smiles and says, "Yes I am, but when I am through, my ditch will join with their ditches to create a trench. Then we will dig three more ditches to join these three and we will continue digging ditches down into that valley below." He points to the valley. "Our ditches become the trench that will hold the pipes that will carry the water that will supply a city that will be built down there. I hope to live in that city. My sons and daughters can go to those schools to learn what I could not, so that they will never have to dig a ditch like their father."

That third man understood meaningful work.

Although we may have to think about how to do it, we can find purpose for our labors in any occupation and at any company. When we do recognize that we have value in doing our jobs, we increase our satisfaction as we do our tasks.

One of modern society's greatest losses is the loss of intrinsic value we place on a job well done. It is a biblical principle that has all but vanished from the workplace today. Even so, finding meaning in our work is still a critical motivating factor for most employees, and a great deal of that meaning *must be intrinsic*. The greatest intrinsic reward I know is the one that comes from doing work that is considered Unconditionally Excellent. Again, I think of Feet Motley who just wanted to make a difference.

5. Community

Even though we are crowded together, we are more isolated than ever before. The change that has taken place in the nuclear family and in our neighborhoods has created a greater need for kinship in places we never thought of as community. Work is one of those places. We spend hours at our jobs, five days a week, alongside others all the time. Organizations that can create and maintain a strong sense of community have more satisfied and more productive employees and a higher rate of retention.

Community is another form of group relationship; building strong relationships is one of the foundational principles of Unconditional Excellence. In subsequent chapters on teams, communications, problem solving, and sponsoring champions, I address the impact these important applied skills have on building strong community at work.

6. Career Growth

Few people are satisfied with where they are in their careers. Part of their dissatisfaction comes from the fact that they see no growth plan, career track, or way out of a career that may be less than fulfilling. The nature of humanity is developmental. We're constantly growing; the same must be true of our careers. We are motivated if we know that we're on a path that provides career advancement.

Given our desires as employees, knowing what satisfies us, isn't it remarkable how seldom we find it at work? Employers could dramatically impact their bottom line if they would find ways for employees to align their personal desires with the goals and objectives of the company. This would fulfill the vision of both.

Is that too impractical? I don't believe so.

The foundational factors of pay, benefits, and job security stand out so much in what employees desire from their careers that the factors with the actual power to transform desires into purpose become less obvious. But even with that, all too often, our personal purposes tend to focus on one question: "What's in it for me?"

I hope the quest for Unconditional Excellence creates a further transformation—that our purpose becomes our personal destiny.

When Purpose Becomes Personal Destiny

Personal destiny is another term that many people struggle with when they first hear it. I was even challenged by my associates at CDI to drop it from our lexicon when we first introduced the seminars several years ago. I considered doing that, but the idea that each of us has a personal destiny—much like the concept that our company should have a vision—just wouldn't go away. Earlier I wrote about the lack of clarity that exists in the vision and mission of many companies. The same is just as true for the employees of those companies. If we don't have a life purpose—that is, a sense of personal destiny—how will we know where we're going?

The six factors I presented are true in the broadest sense for all employees, but each of us needs to determine to what extent each is important for us.

How much meaning do we seek from our work? If our jobs are merely a means to an end, a paycheck, and a few benefits, there is little motivation to learn and apply the principles. If part of our motivation is to clarify our personal destiny and align that with the vision and mission of our company, Unconditional Excellence is the way to do it.

Here's an example of how one man answered the question, "What is your personal destiny?"

David and I sat across from each other at a restaurant. He had asked me to give him guidance in his career decisions. "What do you want from your career?" I asked.

"I'm trying to find a career that allows me to enjoy what I do every day when I wake up. These past few months have been a real drag. I am having a hard time getting motivated and my new boss is the worst boss I've ever had."

David had graduated from college four years earlier. He had married his college sweetheart and would soon be a father. He was a salesman for a relatively large software company, having left a job as an assistant manager at a small audio/video supply company. When he took the sales position, we had discussed his reasons. Foremost in his mind was to increase his potential earnings so he could start a family. They had decided that until their kids were in school, his wife wouldn't continue with her career.

"So the money is excellent, the freedom is good, and your boss is lousy," I said bluntly. "If you still had your old boss, would you like what you're doing?"

"Not as much as I thought I would. The money is far better than I expected. In fact, this year I'll probably make twice what I was making last year. But even with my old boss, I realize that I just don't get as much satisfaction out of selling as I thought I would."

"Okay, let's look at that. The money is exceptional, the benefits are outstanding, and you have job security. Three basics, and yet the job isn't satisfying." I smiled and then said, "For people on the path to Unconditional Excellence, you are at the exact best starting point. The real desire is to transcend your basic needs and find more meaning, community, or opportunity."

"That's right," he said.

David suffered from what many of us go through in our careers, regardless of how long we have been working. In the early stages, he made decisions based largely on financial criteria. Then he felt trapped by that choice. If he acted typically, within a few more years he would develop a lifestyle so dependent on his high income that one day, in deep misery, he would have to say, "I'm not happy, but I'm too far down the road to turn back."

I had several more meetings with David. Each time I pushed him to decide what he liked to do.

Because David and I were both Christians, I could push him even harder. Most Christians believe that God has a purpose or a plan for our being on this earth. Part of our task is for us to open ourselves to that purpose. When we know what it is, we can honestly say that God *calls* us to that task.

"What do you feel God has called you to do?" Once David answered, he could then examine how much money he needed to fulfill his family needs. Several times I helped him to understand that income, although a significant priority, isn't the only aspect of career satisfaction that matters. David could live nicely on less, yet he had continued on with the expectation that he should stay in a job he didn't like under a boss he didn't respect simply because income levels largely drove his personal destiny.

David isn't unique. He isn't even particularly unusual in this regard. I've seen this happen—often—and so have most of us. It's a wonder that I'm not a hundred pounds overweight, given all the breakfasts and lunches I have been invited to just so I could listen to a talented, well-paid executive share the same concerns. "I feel trapped," the executive might say. If they don't actually use those words, that's the message anyway.

My response goes something like this, "You are only trapped when you have no direction, no desire, and no destiny. Once you recognize that you have choices, you can be released to align your career with your life's purpose." Then, for emphasis, I say clearly, "You can discover your personal destiny."

Their eyes usually come alive then. They have hope.

People who stay in jobs solely for financial reasons often find their job becomes their own personal hell, not a place of relevance, personal satisfaction, or meaningful work. It certainly isn't a place God would call them to live as examples.

Most working people want to balance the same wants and needs. Single mothers must balance their need to be there for their kids with the necessity of providing for them. Career-minded people in every occupation have choices to make, and although pay and benefits are important needs, they alone should not determine our choices.

I stress that because if pay and benefits are the highest goals, we can probably get them—and, in doing so, risk damaging the quality of our lives. At best, we will miss the fulfillment of purpose in our lives that gets increasingly important.

Economic factors, but especially September 11, 2001, caused many of us to examine our lives and ask difficult questions. Although some people felt it was a short-term reaction to tragedy, others saw it as motivation for a long-term change in the way we view our careers.

Because David was good at sales, he stayed in that career track, which gave him freedom and allowed him to earn enough to provide a good living for his family. But rather than stay with a company that (in his words) "burned up its sales people," David moved to a different job—and he now calls it his career—with a company that values long-term relationships with its customers. In his previous position, he sold to customers and then turned them over to the technical support people, so he could start over again with a new client. Now, once he sells to customers, he services them and develops the account.

We can learn as well as David did to know what we want from our careers, what provides satisfaction, and what fulfills our needs. If we know those answers, we can develop our personal growth plan for our career, keeping us on track and focused.

The most satisfied and successful employees find meaning, community, and growth in jobs that meet their financial and security needs. Their commitment to align personal destiny with the needs of the company sets them apart from other employees. Together, they set their company apart from other companies.

ROBI—What Employers Want

I've devoted a lot of space to *what we want* from our employers. What do our employers want from us?

If we can create alignment between what our company wants from us and what we want from our career, we create the first level of alignment between company vision and personal destiny. This is particularly helpful in organizations without a clearly defined corporate mission. We can still develop a higher degree of alignment until the company comes to its senses and develops a corporate destiny.

The answer to "What do employers want?" is obvious.

1. They want us to provide a fair day's work for the pay they give us.
2. They want a fair return on the benefits they invest in us.
3. If they give us more benefits, they expect us to provide more productive resources for them to be able to pay for those benefits.

This third item I call the Return on Benefit Investment, or ROBI.

The ROBI that a company receives from an employee is one that too few people accept responsibility for. Unconditional Excellence demands that an employee accept that responsibility or else it isn't Unconditional Excellence.

I am amazed at how poorly we communicate to most employees the need for the company to experience growth, profitability, and productivity if employees are to expect increases in pay, benefits, and especially job security. Secure companies are high-performing organizations, not corporations on the verge of fiscal disaster.

Our leaders want us to have these things because, over time, they make us more productive, which gives the company more security. The way employers offer job security is to provide *company security*—from having secure, long-term relationships with customers to training us to be so employable that, even if the business fails, our skills, our ability, our talent, and our character are in demand anywhere.

Those who follow the guidelines in this book can become the most employable people in the workforce. That's the attitude we want to create. We don't want to worry about a business's lifetime employment policies, because lifetime employment opportunities are our personal responsibility, not that of our employers.

Employers want us to be satisfied. After all, who wants to manage disgruntled, unhappy people? Good leaders want to establish community. Workers who feel as though they are part of a community—people who belong—are more productive and more satisfied in their jobs, which means higher employee retention. When employee retention increases, usually customer satisfaction and retention increases. When we retain the best, most satisfied customers, we can lead our industries in profitability, shareholder value, and long-term stability.

The Need for Community

Most companies are just beginning to understand the word

community. That is, they are beginning to sense that employees need a sense of belonging. People spend so much time at work that they desire to feel as though they are part of something more like an extended family or a close-knit neighborhood than a statistic on a corporate organization chart. As business leaders tap into the concept, they're discovering that through community they get more productivity rather than less.

It is unfortunate, but too many leaders fail to understand this important motivational tool. They understand community as just a "feel good" time-waster. They wrongly conclude that if we have a viable community, we produce less. What if we could turn a sense of belonging and teamwork into greater productivity? If we did, and if we could make it show functionally, companies wouldn't run from community but would actually begin to develop a culture conducive to it.

chapter four

Excellence in Communications

Most of the time, we know what others expect of us and what we can expect of ourselves. We resolve to live up to those standards, and we start with good intentions. Even though they're not usually expressed, these are the qualities and actions that we're sure we'll fulfill:

- My intention is to be the best possible employee I can be for this business.
- My intention is to have an excellent team spirit, with my cooperation, so we never have disagreements or arguments.
- My intention is to become a vital part of this company and to help it serve our customers better than any other organization could.
- My intention is to do everything I can to make sure that everyone who works here is happy, satisfied, and well paid.

There is nothing wrong with good intentions, and we need

to start with those self-commitments. The problem is, good intentions just aren't enough. What happens when our intentions don't fulfill themselves? That is, what happens when we fail to live up to the ideals and standards we have set for ourselves? As we discussed earlier, good intentions will not lead to Unconditional Excellence. Execution will.

Perhaps the best way to show this problem is to look at the matter of communication. When we fail to communicate effectively, no matter how excellent our objectives or desires, we create huge problems. Too often what people hear is our intention, but what they see is our behavior.

Aside from the difficulties that ineffective communication causes, many people—especially our critics—assume that a failure to live up to our intentions means we lack integrity. Failure doesn't necessarily indicate a lack of integrity, but it's still failure.

I once worked for a man, call him Hal, who considered every failure to live up to a committed goal as a reflection on a person's integrity. What happened as a result of his flawed thinking? Knowing that he would see the gap between what they committed to and what they accomplished as a lack of integrity—when it may well have had more to do with poor goal-setting than anything else—his employees began setting lower goals. They were no longer willing to stretch themselves.

"What is your sales goal commitment for the next quarter?" Hal asked me.

"How about 2 percent above last year for the same quarter?"

"You can do much better than that, can't you? Aim higher."

"If I told you my own personal goal was much higher than a 2 percent increase, and then I didn't make it, you would say I had no integrity. So my integrity is safe if I set it low."

Hal didn't understand what I was saying.

When we communicate our commitment to Unconditional Excellence, and we do communicate it, we also need to avoid setting ourselves up for expectations that we cannot deliver.

If we intend to be excellent in the workplace, we need to realize one significant factor: Commitment to Unconditional Excellence is *not* perfection. If these principles are applied they will raise the standard appreciably in individual and company performance, but they will never lead to perfection.

My vice president of quality control at Sklar Pepplar Furniture in Canada stated it well. At a quality team meeting, some of the sales people came with expectations that the product they were selling would ultimately be perfect and free from defects in materials or manufacturing.

"Gentlemen, none of your customers want perfection because their customers will not pay for perfection," Mike said and laughed. "What we offer is excellence. Let's define the standards clearly so we can communicate that to our customers and our employees."

What a great comeback. Commit to excellence. No one is capable of perfection.

Years ago, as I began to teach these principles, my greatest concern was that people would communicate the challenge to

Unconditional Excellence as a commitment to perfection. People who don't understand the nature of God's grace can easily fall into that trap. They make a strong commitment and expect to become perfect in their work. That isn't realistic. Even when we do our best, at times we all fail. We fail as employees, and we fail as employers. In fact, regardless of our intentions, there's no way that we'll ever be perfect.

That's probably obvious. What may not be so obvious is that our commitment to Unconditional Excellence means *failure is not an excuse for giving up the ideal.* We set standards that are constantly moving upward. That is, we keep striving for better job performance, but we always focus on the level we can attain at that stage of our development and ability. If we set standards for ourselves that are too high, we either give up in frustration, or we lower the standards. Most of the time it's the latter.

When we seek to communicate on the basis of our new standard—that of Unconditional Excellence—we need to be aware of what we're doing. We don't set ourselves up to fail by making our goals impossible. And, frankly, if our intention is that we'll raise and maintain the new standard 100 percent of the time, we won't make it every time.

The Foundation of Applied Skills— Communications

In the previous chapter, I pointed out the six things that employees want. The three motivating factors are what I call "communication intensive." Communication is a foundational skill. Before we can develop our applied skills in other areas, we need to increase our skill and ability to communicate using Unconditional Excellence.

I want to share a real situation that, although personally embarrassing, illustrates how widespread the need really is for Unconditional Excellence in communications. I have spent a great deal of my career doing organizational consulting and development. One of the first things that happens in consulting and development is some sort of assessment or evaluation of the current situation. At CDI we call the process the DNA— Developmental Needs Assessment.

Much like a doctor examining the patient, we scrutinize the company using a number of tools, from sophisticated surveys to simple evaluation and assessment interviews. Several years ago, after a particularly rough travel schedule and a very poor night's sleep, I was wrapping up an evaluation session with the CEO of a potential client company.

The CEO turned to me and said, "So what do you think the major problem is?"

My mind went blank. It was something that had never happened to me before. I couldn't even tell anyone what city I was in or the day of the week. Rather than stall for time, I blurted out the first words that came to me. "The problems are threefold: First, you have an unclear vision. Second, your leadership is not aligned. And finally, you have a problem with communication."

He sat back, hands folded in front of him, contemplating my diagnosis. "You know, Alan, you're right."

I am sad to say that this is a true story. Yet I have realized that after more than a quarter-century spent working in hundreds of businesses, it is almost *always* true for organizations that need help. Maybe I never get to see the companies that have a clear vision or aligned leaders, but I'll bet you every CEO in the world would conclude, "We need to improve on our communications." It is a rampant problem in every kind of organizational structure, whether in the corporate or nonprofit world.

That is precisely why communication is the first applied skill we work on. Communication makes the biggest difference in the shortest time. As stated, it is a foundational skill, leading to more dramatic improvement in other applied skills like team building and problem solving.

Meaningful work is communication intensive. We can't have meaningful work unless some form of communication comes from the leadership level to each employee that says, "What you do matters." This message doesn't have to be verbal, nor does it have to be one that the CEO speaks or writes to each person individually. Yet somehow the intentions and values of the company which we work for need to be expressed in a way that each of us understands.

Effective communication skills are at the core of developing a culture where people feel they belong and are accepted as they are. Community comes through relationship building, and that requires effective communication skills. The potential for career growth and opportunity is significantly enhanced if we learn to communicate with Unconditional Excellence. Because so many organizations have communications problems, employees who become part of the solution stand out clearly from the rest of the crowd. I would sooner promote a worker with good technical skills and excellent communications skills over a worker with outstanding technical skills and poor communication. The more we are involved in leading others, the more excellent communication skills we need.

Communicating Unconditional Excellence

One of the first ways we can improve our communications skills is to understand how people interact. We tend to focus on what we write or say, yet the most powerful form of communication a company can establish is based on behavior rather than action.

For seven years I was a partner in a manufacturing company, Design South Furniture, that my wife and I ended up buying outright. We wanted to communicate meaningful work, and we wanted all our employees to feel a sense of belonging and to feel important. We wanted them to grasp that every person who worked there was valuable and that no work was meaningless, even in the least skilled jobs in the factory.

In furniture manufacturing, there are two jobs that I consider the worst. One is the spray-finish booth, and the other is the sanding line.

The spray-finish booth is filled with fumes. It's dirty, and it's messy. No matter how hard factory owners try to vent the area, there is no way to get rid of the bad fumes. We made a significant change that improved the environment, and it was also a mark of Unconditional Excellence. We went from using chemical-based finished material products to a water base, which not only prevented long-term effects on our employees, it was also better for the environment. Not only did it cost our business to implement the change, but the new method was more expensive, which meant if we did not improve quality or volume, it would reduce profit.

The new process cost more money because it meant we had to spray more products. Waste is increased because of the water base, which doesn't adhere as effectively. All furniture manufacturers knew the same as we did when we made the decision to convert to a water-based system. Some changed; others didn't.

Companies that cared about people made the switch long before the Environmental Protection Agency made it mandatory. It was easy to recognize those who cared more about profit than they did about people. When asked why they didn't leave their chemical-based procedure, the stock answer from these companies was, "It would just cost us too much money."

If they didn't switch, what was it costing their employees on the finishing line? Any organization committed to Unconditional Excellence looks out for the health of its employees. Sadly, too many employers wait until they are forced to do the right thing by the government, complaining all the while about the regulations put in place because they are too selfish to self-regulate.

The newer product did not smell as bad—not that it smelled *good*—but our people no longer complained about headaches or dizziness. We also knew that we were making a good decision on behalf of their health and individual well-being. That is a good example of an organizational commitment to Unconditional Excellence. However, organizations can only do so much. Individuals really have the greatest potential to bring about change through these principles.

What about the argument that a decision that was in the best interest of the employees might lead to higher costs and reduced profits? Is that a potentially valid reason for not making beneficial changes? Of course not, but let's examine the additional benefits that are realized when you make a decision like this. As our employees began using the water-based products, productivity increased. Why? First, when we explained the reasons for switching, the entire plant knew that we were a company committed to their best interest. It was an action that spoke volumes about our values. Employee morale improved and productivity increased. We hoped that would offset any additional costs for the new process.

What we did not anticipate was the tangible impact the change would have on productivity from a work force that no longer suffered the negative effects of the old finishes. In short, the employees did not have the end-of-the-day wooziness that was so often the case after eight hours of working with nitrocellulose-based products. The numbing effects of constant exposure—the headaches and the sore throats—meant a less productive work force. The costs of the new product were more than offset by productivity gains, not to mention the fact that quality increased as a result of a more focused worker.

The sanding line was at least as bad, and it may have been even worse, because the process creates a fine dust. At the end of the day, workers' eyelids and most of their bodies were coated with the fine layer of dust. They could shower it off, but they'd sometimes sneeze excessively. Some developed coughs from the dust getting into their lungs. Anyone who already had allergies couldn't work there. Our company used the sanding line as the entry level for new workers.

We did the best we could for the health and safety of our employees. As soon as we learned of ways to better the conditions, we implemented them. Our dust collection system was the best we could buy.

Despite the fact that we were gradually making those two entry-level jobs better, none of us ever saw the work as enviable or enjoyable.

I mention this because we had committed ourselves to be a company of Unconditional Excellence. Once we improved conditions, we had almost no turnover, even among entry-level positions. Unfortunately, there was an unforeseen reaction. The more we improved conditions and reduced turnover, the less opportunities we had to promote the sanders from the entry-level work. This meant that people started at the sanding line, and it looked as if they would spend their entire working years doing that kind of work.

That's when we faced the new problem. Now we had encouraged new employees by telling them that they would soon move upward, but there were no positions for them to move into. How, then, could we make them know they were valuable? If they had the dirtiest job in the factory, how could they feel they were as important to the end product as anyone else?

Most of our furniture was hand-painted, and the entry-level employees seldom saw the finished product. They didn't see the results of someone painting for thirty-six hours on armoires. It was gorgeous artwork that went to customers in Albuquerque and Bangor, but the sanders and spray-booth workers rarely saw that.

Because quality is the combined result of many small actions, it involves hundreds of small decisions from the purchase of quality lumber and first-class sanding materials to excellent design, all the way down to putting the correct shipping label on the box. That means that *everything* every employee does will make a difference. If a sander missed the fine burrs that a saw made in the groove of a chair, those burrs became serious quality problems that were recognized too late. If people step back and think about this, most of them admit that's obvious. How could we make that obvious to all the employees?

We wrestled with the question on the executive level by asking each other, "How are we going to communicate this message?" We considered circulating company newsletters, letters, and memos—all written information.

"It won't work," someone said. "Many of those on the entry-level jobs are poorly educated or functionally illiterate."

He was right. What could we do?

"I have an idea," one of the marketing men said. "Let's show them what the product looks like when it's done and ready for sale in the marketplace."

As soon as he said that, we resonated with his suggestion. We decided that we would take every manufacturing employee, including sanders and spray finishers, to our High Point, North Carolina, showroom. That way they could see what they were helping to construct.

We chartered a bus to take them to the International Home Furnishings Market in High Point. This twice-a-year event displays the newest furniture, and it's the highlight of the season. High Point is also where our largest customer, Furnitureland South, had most of our products on display in a Design South Gallery at the entrance to their store. To our delight, we learned that our gallery would be placed in the center of the largest and one of the best furniture retail stores in America.

We invited all thirty-eight employees in those two entry-level positions—strictly voluntary attendance—and let each one bring a family member. We set it up for a Saturday drive of two-and-a-half hours from Toccoa, Georgia.

Two busloads of employees and family members signed up. They showed up in jeans, just as if they were going to work. Not one of them wore a tie or looked dressed up, and that was fine. Once they got on the luxury coaches, we served them coffee and breakfast. Because so many signed up, we had to charter two Greyhound limousine coaches equipped with all the latest equipment, including video monitors so they could watch movies during the trip.

Once we reached the furniture market, we asked the top sales representatives to escort them in groups of six through the showroom, during the busiest day of the market. We wanted each of them to feel like a VIP—which each was.

"This is the New York of the furniture industry," one of

our people said as he started the guided tour. I could tell from the expressions on the faces of those workers that they enjoyed every part of the tour. Our intention was to make them feel like princesses and princes. We wanted to honor them for their faithfulness to Unconditional Excellence in helping to produce an excellent product. We also wanted *them* to be able to point to a piece of furniture in a store and say, "I helped to make that piece."

As significant as our showroom was, the greatest impact was the Furnitureland South gallery. For one of our previous High Point shows, the design department had created painted panels of scenes from our factory showing people, and some of them were the same people on those buses. Our sales rep for Furnitureland South took those panels and created an incredible backdrop in the middle of our gallery.

As the workers walked through the display area, they saw paintings of themselves. They stared, grinned, and pointed at the pictures of someone sanding or spray-finishing—all-important steps that led to the final product.

We pulled off an outstanding event. It was also a huge communications success and I don't think we printed a single piece of paper or sent out any memos.

That's why I'm including this story. Without having to read a word or listen to someone make long speeches or present awards, they understood we had set a new standard of Unconditional Excellence. Nobody ever forgot that trip.

Those level-entry workers had a powerful, unique experience, and, obviously, it was one we couldn't replicate. Even so, as the owner of that company, I had never gotten more positive feedback than from this event. They understood. They *knew* they were part of a team that committed themselves to Unconditional Excellence.

What did this experience teach me? I realized that communication from the leader to every employee is powerful. It can affect the entire company. This realization has forced me to find creative ways to deliver a message and try to help people experience a vision, rather than just reading it on a plaque in the front hallway.

Here's a second example. One day I visited Truline Industries, Inc., owned by Court Durkalski. It is primarily a one-product company that makes ball bearings.

Court took me around the plant for a tour, personally. Tours are telling experiences for me as an organizational-development fanatic. Time after time, I am amazed that many of the execs conducting the tour know almost everything about the equipment—especially the really fancy, high-tech stuff, and yet they don't know the names of any of the employees that operate the machines. Court not only knew their names, but it was obvious they knew him, too.

The first person I saw was Glen, who was working in a nice cubicle. (His name was stitched on his shirt pocket.) "What work do you do?" I asked. "I make these." Glen pointed to pictures of F-16s and F-22s on the wall behind him. The military aircraft had been photographed taking off from aircraft carriers. Another picture showed them landing. The proud smile on his face made it clear that he meant what he said.

In reality, Glen made the bearings that went into those planes. Some would have said *only* bearings, but Glen had received the right kind of communication. He was doing more than making bearings because he held a position that demanded Unconditional Excellence. There is no room for error in what Glen does.

Without hearing the words, "Every day, quality is our number one purpose, and there's no room for error," he had gotten the message. He had only to glance at the wall and realize that many lives were at stake if he made even a slight mistake. Those pictures and the constancy with which Court communicates the meaning of his employees' work drive their commitment to Unconditional Excellence.

Communications Clutter

Let's look at the day-to-day problems we get into as communicators and how we can increase our skill in applied communications. Part of the great difficulty in the process occurs because we have to deal with a growing problem called "communications clutter." In our lives today there are two components of clutter. One is sender clutter, and the other is receiver clutter.

Because of how busy the world is today and its self-centeredness, we have developed an attitude that says, by our actions if not our actual words, "You think you've got problems. I'm the one with the real problems." The increasing decline of effective customer service is partly due to the amount of communications clutter we have to endure.

The pressure on most of us is enormous. We become over-whelmed with the clutter. That forces us to communicate by expecting that the other person is getting our messages. It's as if we assume they have some kind of mind-reading equipment to understand what we're saying.

Clutter comes in all forms and from myriad sources. It can range from distractions in the cubicle next door, attitudes that begin with a closed mind, being busy, competing priorities, and even something as simple as too many electronic communications devices. For instance, one day when I was talking on my office phone, my cell phone rang. Not thinking, and since I was on hold, I answered that call. The person who had put me on hold came back just as my executive assistant walked into my office and asked me a question—I had to deal with all three simultaneously. Because I also happened to be late leaving for the airport, I had so much clutter that I'm not sure what I said to any of the people involved.

If we don't take into account that communication always involves both sender and receiver clutter, we probably deliver a lot of messages that never get received. Likewise, we probably miss many important messages that are sent to us. Those two components—sender and receiver clutter—can cause any message to be less than excellent.

So what do we do? I'll illustrate how this works. Let's say I'm returning a call to a customer who has encountered a major problem. Even before I begin, I need to assume there's clutter going on in that person's life because I know there is in mine. Her boss may have yelled at her. His wife may be in the hospital and he's more focused on her health than on his work. Perhaps the person feels overworked and is trying to do two full-time jobs.

Because we're usually focused on ourselves—as they are on themselves—we don't take time to say, "I understand this mistake probably caused you a problem." This gives them no chance to disengage from their own convoluted situation. We can do that so easily with a few words, such as, "Is this a convenient time for you?" or "Are you able to talk to me now?" These are remarkably simple questions, but they give the other person the chance to push away from the immediate environment and focus on what needs to be discussed.

Instead of setting the environment for successful communications, we are more like the mealtime telemarketers that go right into their spiel, never once considering whether we're dealing with a meal burning on the stove, a screaming baby, or a ten-guest dinner party.

As a result, the message sent isn't delivered. This is true even if we say what we consider to be clear, concise, and appropriate. It's useless to try to stop the clutter, because we'll never do it. If we can't control the distractions in our own lives, how can we do that for anyone else?

Let's say I've just started a phone conversation with a customer and my boss walks in. He hands me an urgent memo and walks on. I then get a call on the other line. I get an e-mail from a customer I've been waiting to hear from for three days. In the midst of all this, I'm trying to carry on a conversation with an important customer. That's *my* clutter.

As difficult as it is to get through the environmental mess of customers, it is often significantly more difficult to get through it with coworkers or suppliers. We tend to set an order of importance. If customers are at the top and we're already struggling to communicate well at that level, it doesn't offer much hope for those who are on the bottom of that pecking order.

Therefore, it comes down to this: If I can't control the environment in which I'm communicating, I have to control the three things I can do something about. We do this in simple steps.

The Three M's
1. The Message

In communicating to achieve Unconditional Excellence, we first ask ourselves one question: "What is the message I want the receiver to hear?" This isn't the same as asking, "What do I say to this person?" This refers to the *end result* of my communication.

There is so much lack of clarity in the messages that we send today, whether by voice mail, e-mail, or in face-to-face encounters. The whole area of communication becomes a matter of missed expectations because people assume we're going to do something. Unfortunately for us, we don't know what they assume we'll do. When we don't fulfill their unexplained expectations, they wail, "You've failed me." That also implies that we lack integrity because we've promised to do everything we can accomplish and then don't do it.

2. Medium

Once we have answered question number one, question number two is simply, "What is the best medium for delivering that message so that it is received in the way I want it to be received?"

Suppose I'm a supervisor who has to reprimand someone on my team. Is an e-mail the best medium to use? Definitely not. That seems obvious, and yet I'm constantly shocked at how many leaders send e-mail messages to tell an employee, "You have messed up." It is the worst way to reprimand.

Aside from being impersonal (which it is), it can also easily appear that I'm setting up a case file against that person. The employee assumes, "Okay, this is the first of the records that will go into that file she's keeping on me." Worse still is that a reprimand delivered by e-mail is too ineffective to do much good. Cowardly leaders reprimand or rebuke by e-mail.

As bad—or perhaps worse—is if I decide to reprimand by voice mail. "Helen, I'm really disappointed with you because you failed me on that Borden project."

It's a cold message. It allows no room for feedback or human interaction.

All that Helen gets is a brusque voice message, and it clutters up the situation even more. Here are possible questions that go through Helen's mind:

- Is Alan angry with me?
- Is he planning to fire me?
- Was I the one who messed up, or was it Howard and I'm being blamed?
- If I failed, how serious were my mistakes?
- Why won't he let me talk to him and at least try to explain why it happened the way it did?

What is the acceptable way for me to deliver a reprimand? It's the face-to-face, eyeball-to-eyeball approach. It takes place when one human being speaks directly to another in the privacy of an office or across a desk. Now I realize that this may sound rather obvious, but I am shocked at how many bosses today use an electronic medium to reprimand because it's quicker and easier—for the bosses, that is. It's also extremely demoralizing and dehumanizing to employees.

Am I saying that all messages should be given in person? Obviously not, and sometimes that's impossible anyway. That leads us back to the second question: *What is the best medium to send the message?*

I'll start to answer by asking another question: What is the best way to send out factual information? Certainly not by voice mail because as people listen to voice mail they have to be able to write down what I'm telling them. To send factual information, e-mails are excellent. We can send a memo or a brief statement with data content. It's before their eyes, and it can become permanent. I assume we also think carefully about the first question before we click the send icon: *What is the message I am sending?*

Most people would read the paragraph above and say something such as, "Yes, that's obvious." The trouble is, we don't do it often enough, and we don't send the information correctly. I estimate that 90 percent of e-mails are so cluttered that even if they are informational, it takes an immense amount of time to figure out what the information actually is.

If we don't get the message as we skim through the lengthy e-mail (and most of us are so busy that we do skim), we can't respond the way the sender wanted. Later the blame comes when that person asks, "Why didn't you do what I asked?"

"What was that? I had no idea . . ."

"I sent you an e-mail," is the usual, brusque reply. Or maybe he says, "Didn't you read my e-mail?"

The truth is, not only do we skim, most of us don't read to the bottom of e-mails—especially the long ones. Our attention span has gotten so short that we open the message, glance at the first few lines, perhaps skim the next paragraph or two, press delete, and go on to the next message.

Below is an actual e-mail that I sent to Phyllis, my executive assistant. What I got back was completely different than what I wanted. Although I've learned a lot since then, I share this as part of my own learning experience. Until that experience, I prided myself on being a fairly good communicator. I had to learn the hard way—which is too often the way most of us finally learn.

Phyllis,

I need you to ask Chris if he has the preliminary report for the meeting with Myers on the 7th of June. We are not presenting the final report then so I won't need that until the meeting in Akron. We are going to make a presentation based on the findings to Dale and Dana so he needs to have it ready. He'll need to get it to me before the meeting so I can go over it. If Dale and Dana need a ride, we need to arrange a pick up. Will the final report be ready by the 25th in order to prepare for it before the

meeting on the 30th? Chris needs to be available too. You
can go ahead and make the arrangements for both of us.

> *Thanks, you're great,*
> *Alan*

I've given copies of the above e-mail to several people and
then I've asked, "What does it say? What do I want done? What
would you do if you got it?"

In the next example, you can see how that e-mail message
should have looked. This e-mail couldn't possibly be misunderstood: It's clear and clean.

Phyllis,

> *Please help. Background Information: Dana and*
> *Dale will be in Atlanta on June 7th for us to present the*
> *results of the survey. We will follow that up with a June*
> *30th meeting in Akron.*

> *ACTION REQUESTED:*
> 1. *Make sure Chris has the preliminary report to me*
>   *by the 6th.*
> 2. *Let Chris know I need him to be at the meetings*
>   *on the 7th and the 30th.*
> 3. *I need the final report from Chris by the 25th of*
>   *June.*
> 4. *Please make our travel arrangements for the*
>   *Akron trip.*

Please call Julie at Myers to see if Dana and Dale
need to be picked up at the airport.
If so, please arrange a limo.
Thanks, you are great,
Alan

As embarrassing as it is, I wrote both of those e-mails. The first one was the real e-mail, the one I expected my efficient executive assistant, Phyllis Rice, to read, understand, and act on. When Phyllis came into my office the next day with the e-mail in her hand, her way of getting my attention was excellent. She placed a printed copy of the e-mail in front of me and said, "What do you think this crazy man wants?" (Both of us knew she was referring to me.)

I had written the e-mail so I read it twice, shook my head, and said, "I have no idea." Sheepishly, I wrote message number two.

3. Motivation

For some, the third *M* may not be quite as obvious as the first two. Motivation asks, "What kind of action do I want? What do I want the receiver to do?"

- When I send an e-mail, what do I want the recipients to do?
- Do I want them to skim, delete, and do nothing?
- Do I want them to read it and then save the e-mail to cover themselves if something goes wrong? (And we do have to do that in business.)

- Do I want them to file it because they might need to refer to it later?
- Do I want them to act on the information today?
- Do I want them to act on the information later?
- Do I want them to gather information and send it back to me so that I can complete what I need to do?

We can't work as a team effectively unless we communicate effectively. We'll mess up what we're trying to do. Worse, people won't realize that these are communication flaws. They'll tend to see them as character flaws.

So first, we need to ask, "What is the message?"

Second, based on that message, we ask, "What medium should we use?"

Third, based on the medium chosen, we ask, "How should I structure the message so that the person who reads it will be motivated to do what I want?"

I'll illustrate this with the use of voice mail. Because of the almost universal deployment of voice mail, e-mail, and text paging, communication has changed drastically, even though we haven't always changed with it. We've assumed that those media didn't alter anything about how we convey a message or attempt to motivate someone—except, perhaps, to accomplish them faster. But those forms have changed communication forever, especially in the business world.

Suppose I call Ron and reach his voice mail. I say, "Hi Ron, this is Alan. Oh, will you hold a second? Someone just walked in." I pull away from the phone, greet the person, listen as she briefly explains what she wants, and I say to the visitor, "Oh, sure, yeah, I'll get that for you." Then I go back to the voice mail. "Oh, Ron, how are you doing? I hope you had a good trip to Wisconsin. My trip to Portland was extremely productive." Even though my Portland trip is not germane, I ramble on and tell him about a trip that had nothing to do with him. "Oh, Ron, I'm going to be traveling, uh, I'm going to be out of town and there's a couple of things I need to get for you but, hold on just a second."

When he listens to this garbled voice mail, he will be confused by my distracted information. My clutter level is getting in Ron's way. Ron is stuck, waiting to know what I really want. If Ron works for me, he will persist until he understands what I want, even if he has to replay it four times. If Ron doesn't work for me, by now he has likely hit the delete button. I would.

"Well, uh, so Ron, I'd like you to, if you don't mind, would you get back to me and let me know what it is I need to do in order to be ready for Monday?" I stare at a note on my desk that momentarily distracts me. "Uh, sorry. I'm going to be traveling. Yeah, uh, I'm going to be out of town. It's going to be hard to get me because I'm going to be at a hotel. I don't know which one exactly. Well, the hotel I'm staying at is in California. I'm not sure if it's the Hilton, or maybe it's the Ramada. I don't have the number right now. I don't think my cell phone will work out there. Can you get back to me on that and that way I can be prepared on Monday? Okay?"

After listening to that voice message, Ron says to himself,

"Hmm, I think I know what Alan wants—I mean, basically I know, but I still don't know what to do with it." He wastes at least five minutes replaying my voice-mail message. At the end he's still as confused as when he first played it.

Here's a better version of my voice mail. "Hey, Ron, this is Alan. I'm going to be going out of town all of this week, but Phyllis is here in the office. Will you e-mail me the specific things I need to know and do so that I can be ready to make my presentation on Monday for the Bates Company? She will give it to me. I'm not quite sure where I'm staying, or if you can get in touch with me, but Phyllis is prepared to e-mail it to me if you'll e-mail it to her.

"Here's what I need. First, can you send me the original proposal? Would you also send me any changes you made? There's something in the proposal about taking some of the material and doing it in half the space. Could you give me your thoughts on that? Thanks. Hope you're having a great day." Then I hang up.

My message is clear to Ron. He knows what I want and he's motivated to respond. This is clear communication.

When we talk about clear communication, it means not only that we're clear in what we say, but also that we're clear about the results we want or expect. We also avoid rambling or getting off on minor issues.

In fact, think of this as our first goal: We tell the other person exactly what we want done.

Here's another significant point. State the action expected as soon and as clearly as possible.

If I want someone to call me back, at the beginning of the message—before I even explained what I want—I'd say, "This is Alan. Can you call me back at 555-641-1970?" Then I'd deliver my message—briefly. Unless it involves the person doing something to get what I need, it may be wise not to explain what I need.

Isn't it amazing how many people leave a voice mail to return their call but no number? The worst is the person who leaves a voice mail that says, "This is Carl. Please call me," and then he hangs up. There is no return number. Worse, I know at least seven people with that first name, so which one is it? If I don't recognize the voice, I have absolutely no clue as to which Carl has called.

My experience—and that of most busy people—is that we tend to call immediately without listening to the rest of the words. Most of the time, I'm going to hear the message repeated when I call anyway.

It's very frustrating, isn't it?

Let's take this a little further. Let's assume I know which Carl has called, but I still have to look up his number. If he had left his number, it would have been much easier, and I could have called back immediately without wasting time. My mood would have been much lighter as well.

This works similarly with e-mails. If someone is going to leave me an e-mail, I want to know at the beginning—preferably in the first sentence—what that person wants from me.

Code Words

In response to this very problem, we started a system here at CDI with code words, so that anyone in our office knows exactly what the sender means and what the motivation is.

If I send an e-mail, there are four possible things the receiver does with it and he or she will know from the subject line.

1. FYI Discard

This means the e-mail is for Tony because I want to keep him informed. He won't need to refer to the information again. E-mail jokes come under this category along with "just stuff." By the way, that isn't an endorsement for e-mailing jokes— another huge clutter-creator.

2. FYI File

This isn't important today, but Tony may need it for reference or to settle any questions that may arise. This means, "Keep this on file where you can retrieve it."

3. Action

When anyone at CDI gets e-mail with that designation from any of us, he or she will be expected to act on that information. If it's just Action, then we can decide when we're going to do it. We can do it today or we can do it later.

4. Action for Team

This means one of two things: I'm holding somebody up if

I don't act immediately, or I need to get with someone to complete this action. I cannot respond alone. I need help, or someone else on the team needs mine.

Now that these four codes have become part of our standard procedures, it's amazing how quickly I go through my messages. When I spot FYI, I tend to wait and read them later. They also tend to be the longer messages.

If my assistant, Phyllis Rice, sends me *Action for Team*, she's telling me what she wants from me, and I understand that someone else is waiting for an answer from me through Phyllis. That someone else can't do what needs to be done until my response comes. This enables me to be clear and Unconditionally Excellent.

Crisis Communication

As I've pointed out, none of us can control the clutter in our lives. We can become intuitive enough to understand the simple steps of how to leave an easy-to-follow voice mail or a clear e-mail message.

What we need to be careful of is situations where we're sending the message into a place of ongoing crisis. In these cases, the receiver may be so fear-filled that he unintentionally distorts the message.

For instance, Margaret works in accounting. She's just gotten all the requests for payment for expenses from Harry. She e-mails him and says, "I need you to justify your bill from

Harrison Brothers." That's all she writes.

How does Harry respond? Maybe he's already a little insecure. That message makes him feel threatened. Harry will need to give Margaret enough information to save his job. What he sends may not be what Margaret wants or what she had in mind, but after he goes through all his own clutter, he assumes that's what he needs to do.

Margaret violated all three *M's* of communication. The problem began because she used the wrong medium. She compounded it by sending the wrong message. She also committed a third fatal error because she didn't make the motivation clear. Maybe she thought she told Harry what action she wanted, but she really didn't. So why should she be surprised if she gets Harry motivated to act in a way that she's not asking for?

Here's a basic rule to bear in mind when communicating: *Fear and crisis tend to cloud everything.* The message sent—no matter how well articulated—can't always break through fear- or crisis-based clutter.

On the other hand, people who are Unconditionally Excellent in communication can learn to sense the fear or crisis that lurks. Because they begin with the right attitude and then answer all three of the *M* questions before they start their messages, they can usually break through the clutter.

For example, I like to communicate with people who take the time to say, "Alan, I know that you guys must be buried right now. Is there anything that I can do to take something off you?"

"No, you really can't at this point," I'll probably say. I may add, "Can we delay this?" I can ask that question because that person has broken through my clutter by being sensitive to my immediate crisis. It is just that simple.

Here's an example. I had arranged for my cowriter, Cec Murphey, to come to my office to work on this book. He walked in, spotted the mess on my desk, overheard the tension in my voice as I spoke on the phone, and observed my body language. "Is it better for you if we don't do this today?"

I cite this because it's an example of Unconditional Excellence in communication. We had a 9:00 A.M. appointment, and he was on time. He observed me, resonated with my situation, and broke through my clutter—and there was a lot of clutter going on. His simple question of concern forced me to look at my situation and make a quick decision.

"No, we can do it today," I said. Once I made that decision to work with him, I had broken through my clutter.

The clutter is still there after the break comes, but we put it behind us and temporarily disengage from it. When we stop long enough to think about the other person and his or her need, we dramatically open the door to full communication. We show our concern with their clutter—and that concern, strangely enough, is one of our most powerful methods of helping them jump over their own barriers.

This leads me to an important principle: When communication works right, we're ready to use all of our competency skills in our move toward Unconditional Excellence. If we can't leap over the barrier of communication clutter, our ability and competency count for little.

In the chapters that follow I write about our character; but if we can't communicate effectively, character becomes a moot point. As those who desire to be Unconditionally Excellent in everything we do, we need to continually remind ourselves that communication is the core of everything else we do.

chapter five

A Community of Teams

The illustration of flying geese has been used hundreds of times, but it's one of the best explanations I've ever heard about teamwork. They fly in a V-shaped, or wing formation. I read that by flying in a wing formation, they create a lift effect that is as high as 73 percent near the end of the formation, where the weakest geese usually fly. The leading geese support the weakest simply because they begin the lift process.

Watching them fly, I used to say to my children, "You know why geese honk so much? It's because they're saying to the leader, 'You're doing a great job, Fred.'"

Fred, I would point out, was the one pushing through and creating the first lift that helped everybody behind him. Fred, the lead goose, needed the encouragement because although he creates the beginning of the lift effect, Fred receives no lift benefit from the wing formation.

Another interesting fact strikes me about this formation. One goose never leads all the way. If we were to watch for several hundred miles as a gaggle of geese flew southward from Minnesota, we'd notice that they keep changing leaders. The point position is extremely tiring. The lift that the wing picks up allows them to fly enormous distances. It's also why geese need to stay together. The weaker ones won't make it if they can't stay in the formation.

This leads me to a question: If a bunch of birdbrains get it, why can't we understand how the godly principle of team effectiveness really works. The original disciples formed one of the most effective teams ever to walk the face of the earth, and they learned it from the best teacher.

I have worked in, formed, broken up, and wished I had broken up as many teams in my lifetime as anyone else I know. Yet I am still amazed at how little we know about teaming and the power teams create.

For several years I worked with Pat MacMillan, founder of Team Resources, an Atlanta consulting firm. Since our name was synonymous with team building, we had many opportunities to create, lead, and teach teams how to work well together.

One client, the CEO of a successful design and construction firm, asked us to develop a new team sales approach for his sales force. He believed that several factors—the complexity of their selling process, their rapid growth and the resulting expansion of their sales force, the need to increase their selling effectiveness—made team-selling a natural.

I conducted an assessment of the sales force, talked to the senior management in the sales and marketing department, and concluded that a team sales approach would be disastrous for them. Their best sales representatives were eagles. Eagles don't flock very well. We can try to make them flock, but they just don't take to it naturally. Eagles like to soar. What they really needed was a good mentoring-and-development program that would get the younger eagles soaring more rapidly. Teams would have added little to the younger staff's effectiveness and would have destroyed the mature sales representatives' effectiveness.

I share this with you because there is a popular misconception that teams work so well that most of our work should be done in teams. Rule number one about teams is this: *"Never create a team for a task that an individual can do faster, better, and cheaper."*

Unconditional Excellence in Teams

We use the team wheel (as shown) to illustrate the critical components that every Unconditionally Excellent team must have.

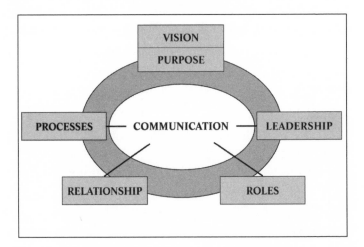

Alignment to a Shared Vision or Purpose

In almost everything written about teams, the experts and authors start with some form of *shared vision*. They may express it in different ways, such as common purpose, common focus, or aligned vision, but the essence is the same. To team with Unconditional Excellence we must have this alignment to some shared goal or purpose.

One of the greatest biblical truths we don't seem to grasp is that we are *interdependent* people. God created us to work in unity, not in isolation. We human beings are created in the image of a triune God, the first and only perfect team.

I'll show you an example of when this *doesn't* work. I had the unpleasant experience of working with an executive leadership team at a company I'll call Bolton Manufacturing. We did a DNA, a survey that tells us a number of things about a company before we start working with them. Barry, the CEO, told me he thought he had a well-focused and aligned team. However, our survey indicated the company had anything but alignment to a shared vision.

Barry was semiretired and wanted things to keep going as they had been, without too many demands on his time and attention, despite the fact they had lost money for the past eighteen consecutive months.

His brother Frank, who had little interest in the business, wanted to spend more time on his favorite pastime—flying. Frank was the only senior engineer on the payroll; if Bolton Manufacturing was going to grow, it had to emphasize engineering.

Mack, the vice president of manufacturing, believed all of the company's problems were due to a lack of concerted effort on the part of the sales group, despite the fact that thirteen of the last fifteen orders had been completed late or with serious rework needed to correct deficiencies. With a little more volume, he was sure he could get things moving along. He thought Larry from sales should be fired.

Larry, the vice president of sales and marketing, believed the company's quality problems were the result of its failure to hold people accountable for their mistakes. Until the company fixed existing problems, his sales people were reluctant to bring in any new business. Larry thought Mack should be fired.

Finally, Richard, the CFO, felt frustrated with all of the leaders because they couldn't work together to solve problems. They all seemed to pull in their own directions with no common goals or purpose. He wanted to see all of them fired.

I asked the CEO, Barry, what he expected us to help him with. He thought they knew their direction, but, in his words, "The team could use a few tools to help them get through the current downturn."

All the tools in the world couldn't have fixed their problems. They had no common purpose and no vision capable of compelling each other, let alone encouraging the rest of the employees to work together for success.

Executive leadership teams are potentially the most powerful, effective, and profitable teams in any business. All too often, however, the same problems we observed at Bolton are what we find in companies, departments, and divisions or offices everywhere. Until the leadership team is in alignment, nothing positive can happen.

I want to examine alignment more closely. The following illustration below represents the typical alignment problems we find on most teams.

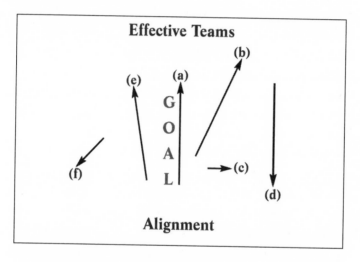

In the diagram, each of the arrows represents various individuals and points to the goals each individual wants to reach.

Which is the most dangerous person to team alignment?

Most people answer *d* because it's diametrically opposed—180 degrees from *a*. Some say, "It's *c* because it's 90 degrees off." Then *c, f,* and *b* all are clearly the same, and there's misalignment. With *c* and *d* we know at the start that they're misaligned so there's no sense in going forward.

The answer is *e,* which *looks* as if it's aligned when it's not. That makes it the most dangerous because in the beginning we think that person is aligned with us. We don't recognize the misalignment until we get a distance down the track.

The other misalignments we spot immediately; that makes *e* dangerous. If we start off wrong we won't end up where we thought we were going—even though we assumed we were properly aligned when we began.

It's easy to tell that someone strongly disagrees when there's a difference of 90 degrees. I can understand and possibly even work with those who are mildly opposed—those at a 45-degree angle. The people I don't recognize as threats or problems are those who are only a few degrees off from my position. If we don't examine the chart closely, it will seem as if we're going in the same direction—but we aren't.

Before we lead or become part of a team, we need to make absolutely certain that all of us understand our common purpose. The question we have to answer is quite simple: What do *we* want to accomplish?

Our united goals must be clear for another important reason. If we know the reason we are teaming, we know the team type best suited to accomplish the objectives.

Functional Teams

Functional teams are part of the hierarchy of any business, built into its ongoing structure. The executive leadership team (or ELT) is a concept that many companies use to provide overall vision, strategy, and planning for their business. All members of this permanent and functional team are the leaders in the major divisions or departments.

Examples are teams for production planning, quality support, customer service, and hundreds of others necessary to plan and execute the functions that support the business. The element common to all functional teams is the responsibility members have for implementing team decisions through their own functional departments or areas. For instance, an accounting supervisor on the Information Technology Support Team would be responsible both for bringing accounting department issues to the team and for executing team decisions in the accounting department.

Usually, functional teams are permanently wired into the structure of the organization. Like departments or divisions, they can be reorganized.

Task Teams

The task team—people from different disciplines within the company or department brought together to complete a specific assignment—is the most productive and powerful kind of team. By design, task teams aren't permanent fixtures. (When I examine barriers to team effectiveness, I'll show the crucial need for a temporary and fixed-time task team.) They may be cross functional with people from different departments and disciplines. They may also represent a number of hierarchal levels within the organization, including for instance a manager from one department and a production employee from another. The more functional and hierarchal diversity we create, the greater the potential to bog down in the politics of power, but diversity also brings the potential for outstanding accomplishments.

I want to focus on the important components that any of us can apply immediately with relative ease. Rather than concentrate on why we form teams, how they're formed, or the impact they can make on the vision, strategy, planning, and execution within a company, I want to focus on two things:

1. What does it mean to be a team member?
2. How can we make a contribution to Unconditional Excellence through teams?

Leadership

Amazingly, many experts leave out a critical component, acting as if a team can be led collectively. Worse yet, they assume the purpose will provide the leadership.

That's wrong.

Tasks don't lead people. People lead people.

Team leadership comes in two basic formats: task leadership and process leadership. Task leaders direct others on component pieces of the objectives. Process leaders keep the whole team on task, focused, and working toward the completion of the team goal.

When I teach these principles, I often hear the comment that task team leaders are similar to subcommittee chairs. I prefer to call them task teams because they focus entirely on the accomplishment of their purpose, while subcommittees tend to concentrate on the members of the committee. Some great task leaders may lead a team of one, but they get the job accomplished. They may provide a level of leadership that supports the team while not leading the team itself.

Team leadership is focused on keeping everyone moving ahead, accomplishing their objectives, and deploying resources wisely.

- The leader of a functional team is normally the functional leader.
- The leader of the executive leadership team is normally the chair, CEO, or president.
- The team leader of the production planning team is usually the plant manager or production manager.

Task teams provide an opportunity for people to develop their skills and to experience leadership by leading. Too many employees who are doing an excellent job in their current position end up doing a terrible job in a new leadership position because they had no practical experience. Task team leadership should be a prerequisite to functional experience.

Task teams have unique leadership dynamics. Many times, the authority to lead comes more from the authority granted by team members than from a position of authority. That can work both positively and negatively. I have seen effectiveness decreased in instances where a team withholds the authority from the leader, despite the fact that the boss might have assigned that authority.

As a young manager, I was asked to participate on a task team assigned to implement an organizational development program called "Compete To Win." My company, Pennsylvania House Furniture, had committed more than a million dollars and a lot of time and energy to make this program a top-to-bottom success throughout the company. My team was assigned to coordinate all of the training. The process we were to keep on track was threefold: assessment of the barriers to our effectiveness, development of a plan to address and eliminate those barriers, and development of a training plan to take the process all the way through the company.

Gary, the head of my team, was the vice president of manufacturing and rumored to be the next CEO. Reg, the vice president of sales and marketing, was my direct boss and a competitor of Gary's for the CEO position. I was one of two direct reports to Reg that he made certain were a part of Gary's team. At first we felt honored and excited. But what became increasingly apparent was that the success of this process was a threat to Reg, especially since his competition, Gary, would look like a hero if he led the task team that made the program work. I assumed the CEO had given him this role precisely to prepare him to take a larger corporate role, as few people outside of manufacturing had much experience with him.

Through us, Reg did everything he could to derail the process. At one point I felt as if I were in a total no-win situation, the most onerous position of all. Every time we attempted to address the lack of unity in the sales and marketing department, I felt disloyal to Reg, my boss, and sensed that I had climbed out alone on a shaky limb.

It was hard to give authority to Gary for fear that Reg would find out. Holding back was very difficult for everyone because sales and marketing was what drove that company.

After months of watching the problem get worse, I approached Gary with my dilemma. To his credit, he protected me from Reg's wrath, allowed me to participate to the best of my abilities, and tried to resolve the problem at the executive level without making my input part of his political advantage.

Eventually, Reg won and Gary left the company. Eight months later, I left because I was unable to work for a man like Reg. To this day I believe that it was partly *our fault* that Reg won and that a good leader and excellent future CEO like Gary had to resign. I am certain that if we had given Gary the authority, things would have been different.

I use this illustration because the politics involved in cross-company task teams can make it difficult for a member to serve one leader while serving under the functional leadership of another. Here are two questions this poses:

1. Do I represent the team to my department or my department to the team?
2. Am I there to protect or am I there to participate?

Team leaders are responsible for helping every team member feel comfortable with dual reporting roles while serving on their teams. Otherwise, corporate politics can destroy any potential positive outcome.

Roles

The first role we need to understand is that of leadership. After leadership roles are clear, we can look at the expectations of other team members.

Besides leadership, there are three primary roles that we can play as a team member.

1. Representative Roles

In most team experiences, members represent their functional area of expertise. For instance, someone from the accounting department would represent accounting expertise, and a person from production would represent production expertise. This can work in both directions. On some task teams, a member may play the representative role from the department to the team and may also be the functional leader that represents the results to the department.

The role of representative is often a fiduciary one. As representatives, we don't represent our interests, but the collective good of the department. People who are highly opinionated or poor consensus builders tend to play this role poorly; they use the power of their representation to put forward personal agendas. Usually we don't see the problem until the team results are reported back to the functional area. Then everyone becomes angry because the representative didn't represent the interests of others in the department.

2. Research Roles

Every team needs information to make decisions. All

members bring information from their own areas of expertise, but there is another task that requires team members to gather additional information, whether within or outside of our functional area.

Lorie Yauney is the director of corporate development at the J. Smith Lanier Company (JSL). She is excellent at selecting task team members with the willingness and ability to do research. We use task teams at JSL to do much of the planning and development work, within functional areas and especially across functional areas. I have never worked with a team that Lorie has put together that didn't have at least three outstanding researchers on it. Consequently, those teams have produced excellent results.

3. Process Roles

Process is a component of teamwork. Process roles are the individual responsibility of team members. If I am responsible for team communication, my process role is communicator. If Lois is responsible for premeeting preparation, then her process role will have an impact on the effectiveness of our meetings if she doesn't do her job well. There are too many process roles to be covered here, but once a team is formed, the task is assigned, and the other roles are clarified, the process roles become clear.

What must be clear about roles is that every member must play multiple positions for the team to succeed. Roles also have a lot to do with the leader's personal skills, abilities, and areas of giftedness. As a team leader you want to assign tasks to people with a natural tendency to succeed. If, as a functional team leader, you want to stretch your people, you can assign jobs that require them to go beyond their personal comfort zone to accomplish those tasks. At the same time, you don't want to risk the success of the team because you wrongly assign a task to a team member.

Relationships

Unconditionally Excellent teams are built on a foundation of strong, mutually rewarding relationships, and the accomplishment of a worthy objective is the most important relationship builder. *The best, strongest, and longest-lasting relationships come through team accomplishment—not team-building exercises.*

Because of my role in organizations, when I discuss the most effective team-building exercises, I always say, "Accomplish anything worthwhile, and you will build relationships. It doesn't have to be your overall task, but it can be a small accomplishment along the way toward the goal. It works far better than anything else you can do."

Here's another piece of advice I offer: "You can also build strong relationships if you commit to Unconditional Excellence *as a team* before you learn and apply the principles in this book. Because these principles are biblically based, they will also be relationship-based."

Every team I have ever led, deployed, or taught that accomplished or exceeded its objectives is a team that developed good relationships among the individual members and also collectively as a team.

Processes

The procedure that functional teams follow to accomplish their work tends to consist of day-to-day business processes. Task teams may develop unique methods based on their task, the team makeup, and the timing and resource requirements of the team.

Following is a list of processes that most teams need at one time or another. What amazes me is that many teams take little time to establish clear processes before they begin their work together. It usually takes a crash-and-burn experience along the way before they go back to basics and try to establish effective processes for team excellence.

The best illustration of establishing clear processes is the checklist a pilot and copilot go through before the plane leaves the gate. At some point, the entire crew is involved in the processes. "Flight attendants, departure check." That's merely a standard process they go through to make sure we are all safe and the doors and evacuation slides are secured.

Processes every team should discuss and consider:

1. Meeting Processes
- Time parameters for meetings, including dates, length, and frequency
- Agenda preparation and communication
- Premeeting checklists
- Meeting logistics, including location, setup, refreshments, materials, and presentation needs

2. Communication Processes

- Team member to team member, leader to team, team to external, and external to team
- Written follow-up requirements and documentation
- Pre- and postmeeting information
- Absentee communication

3. Tracking and Accountability Processes

- Milestone tracking and review
- Objective monitoring
- Team member accountability
- Absentee and failure-to-perform actions

Mutual Accountability as a Process

Teams need mutual accountability. This is a major factor in promoting Unconditional Excellence. Let's say that I am the leader and I have put together a task team and a sales team. Suppose I say to the sales people, "We're going to go after a big account." How do we go about that with mutual accountability?

Here's something that happened to Kevin Davis at Rand Technologies. He was the sales team leader. One thing troubled Kevin. Unlike the others who were on salary, Rand Technologies paid Kevin a commission, and he made more money than any of the others.

Kevin thought about the situation and finally went back to his boss. "This will work a lot better if we had mutual accountability."

"What do you mean?" asked a startled boss.

"If I'm successful at landing this account, I'll make a lot of money, but what about them? They get nothing extra." Kevin asked for his boss to work out some kind of mutual reward system. "That way, all of us can benefit and everybody wins."

Kevin's boss agreed and they changed the pay plan.

The other members of the team felt affirmed and encouraged and put their best efforts into the task. They won the big account.

Think about what happens after a situation like this. When Kevin was ready to work with another team, can't we imagine that everyone wanted to be on his team? When they worked with him, they had added financial incentives to perform with excellence.

It became obvious to everyone that Kevin had the most aligned support team in the organization. The engineers that worked with Kevin also joined others on different tasks. When they joined Kevin, however, he always got the best from them. Not surprisingly, his team always came up with the best solutions.

At the first team meeting, Kevin made certain everyone understood the concept of mutual accountability. "If you don't do your job, I can't do mine." Usually, he would point to one man and say, "If you don't do your job," then, pointing to a woman across the table, "she can't do hers." Everyone got the message.

Kevin understood that when he created mutual accountability, he also helped to create a team. "When the team wins, everyone wins," Kevin said.

This example also shows an excellent way to figure out if

we have the makings of a good team—before the group starts to work together. If someone wins and another loses (or simply doesn't win as much), there is no team. Instead, we have a group of people thrown together by management for some purpose—which may or may not get done.

"I win only if everybody wins." If all the members can make that statement, we have a team. It's not only mutual accountability, but it's also a powerful way to realize that we need each other.

Obviously, the list of processes could go on and on. For the most part, the list above, coupled with a review of each of the components, will go a long way to creating team excellence whether you are leading a team or serving as a member on one.

As little as I care for sports analogies, the best example for developing effective processes comes from the game of football. The game plan and the practice plans are designed to help the team win on game day. No matter how many outstanding individual athletes a team has, overall excellence during the game requires effective, cooperative preparation and process planning.

Communications

In an earlier chapter, we looked at the communication foundation for Unconditional Excellence. I named a number of skills that were communication intensive. Teamwork is one of the most communication-intensive skills. This skill requires not only good written, verbal, and listening skills, but group members constantly need to understand and apply the three *M's* of communication.

It helps to consider that when we work in teams, the channels of communication take on a geometric complexity, adding another layer of potential problems. If you and I are communicating, one channel of communications is all we need to worry about. I worry about my three *M's* and you worry about yours. I consider your clutter and you consider mine. Now let's add another person and we become a three-member team. We have increased the channels to six:

1. Me to you and you to me.
2. Me to her and her to me.
3. You to her and her to you.
4. Me to the team and the team to me. (Believe it or not, we all communicate differently in a group than we do one-on-one. The dynamics have changed; thus, the channels have changed with them.)
5. You to the team and the team to her.
6. Her to the team and the team to her.

We have moved from one channel to six just by adding one person to our communication structure, and the complexity continues to increase geometrically every time we add another member.

I'll show how this works. I met with three of the finest men I've ever worked with, each of whom is responsible for a large division of a family-owned business. Tim is the head of one operating company, Jim heads the second, and Mark runs the management company that supports both operating companies.

Every Monday they have an executive team meeting with John, their father. John is the chair of the entire organization, even though he isn't actively involved in the business except for these Monday meetings. Tim had an insight on the communication aspect of those meetings: He thought the three of them changed the way they communicated when John was in the room.

"Is it better or worse?" I asked.

"It's not really better or worse. Just different," he said.

"It's not as effective when John is in the room as it is when he isn't," Mark added. "I think we are so careful around him that we don't really understand that how we communicate with each other is affected."

"When Dad is in the room, we focus our words based on the impact we think it has on him," Jim said. "I think it is out of our love and deep respect. After all, he is the one who started it all and the one who taught us."

I thought it was interesting that Jim was the only one who called him dad. Even that subtle difference in the relationships between the individuals can influence communications in a marked way.

One of the things we agreed to do as a result of their revelations was to rotate the purpose of those meetings. One would be focused purely on a business review with Tim leading. Changing the leadership and purpose for the meeting added another level of communication complexity to the team process.

Out of our discussion, all three stated that the experience made them realize that they needed to pay more attention to the communication dynamics of the team.

In contrast to the example of those three men, I would say that most teams begin a meeting by saying, "This is where we ended up last time, and this is where we are now." Then the team leader starts talking about what we need to do next.

Here's a better way to start off. "What has happened since our last meeting? How are we doing as a team?" (Notice the question isn't, "*How* are we doing in the task or the purpose?") Here are several questions to ask for the first ten or fifteen minutes of any team meeting:

- Do you feel as if you're being served?
- Do you think communications are good?
- Do you believe everybody's tracking?
- Do we have people who have completed their work ahead of the others?
- Are we moving at the right pace and accomplishing the milestones we set for ourselves?
- What can we do to improve the way we work together as a team?

By taking the time to communicate effectively at every meeting, we avoid the bad habits that tend to create obstacles or rabbit trails in the future.

At its best, the team functions as the most powerful, synergistic, productive performance force we have in business today. Too often, however, those who have the power to build powerful teams seem the least committed to do so.

Consulting firms exist to build teams. Many have built their careers on the principle of teaching team building, yet the people most capable of making a difference seem like the ones bent on remaining independent rather than interdependent.

When people of faith get involved in criticizing, belittling, manipulating, and judging—instead of leading and serving on teams—we become ineffective (or even destructive) members because we're not focused on the good of the entire group. There is a selflessness that is required to be a truly effective team member, a commitment to follow the example of Jesus.

There is a powerful story of how Jesus handled a self-centered, each-man-for-himself situation. When his twelve followers began to argue over who was greater or more important, Jesus did an unusual thing. He got out a towel and basin of water and went around and washed the feet of each man. In those days, the lowest servant or member of a household had that odious task. Jesus set the example. If we are willing to "wash the feet" of others—that is, to serve them—we can become a powerful team.

Releasing Collective Brilliance

Excellent teams breed interdependence. In our American society, we like to think of ourselves as independent, and we focus on *me* and *my*. "I got mine, you get yours."

I have what some may call some startling news. John Wayne died a long time ago, and he hasn't had a replacement. In fact, John Wayne never did anything single-handedly anyway. If we view his World War II films, he never saved the Philippines from the Japanese or put up the flag by himself on Iwo Jima. He had a team—in fact, many support teams.

When teams work right—when they invest in and recognize their interdependence—something exciting takes place. It's called synergy, and it brings about a powerful transformation. It proves the old saying that none of us is as smart as all of us.

When we commit to each other, we can effectively accomplish our purpose. That's what the marketplace screams for. It wants productivity and quality. As those who seek to be bright lights in darkness, we can become the most productive employees in any company.

Why not? Aren't we the ones who know how to bring the power of God into the business world through the power of teams?

Supergluing Teams Together

As I have worked on teams and led them, I've asked myself whom I value the most. The best leaders may be effective team leaders. *Or they may not be.*

From my observations, it's not the leader who makes the biggest difference. It's not the tactical person either—those with professional skills. We need them, but they're generally replaceable, because they come and go and we plug them in where we need them. If they don't function well, we can get rid of them and bring in another person.

There is one type of person that no successful team functions well without. That is a *glue person*—the individuals who bind teams together. They're often the most humble and don't constantly call attention to themselves. What they do—often without recognition—is discover and bring out the best in others. They're the ones who build on relationships. Frequently, they lead from the side or from behind. Rarely do they stand out in front of everyone else.

Why are they so important? That's easy to answer. Glue people model Unconditional Excellence by their character and through their competency. This shows because they have the ability to hold teams together during difficult times.

Maybe it helps to explain this negatively. Without their influence and stability, here's what happens. When a crisis hits or the fear factor creeps in, the sense of unity or togetherness is often the first thing to go. Factions point fingers and members become distracted and distanced from their group goal. Worse, instead of thinking of the team, each one silently asks, "What's best for me?" The team no longer stays in focus.

The glue people hold firmly to others in times of conflict and disruption. In their unique ways, they enable the team to move forward.

At the beginning of this book, I mentioned the men's group I was part of with Nick Richardson, Kevan Sears, and Randy Macall. Each of them was a valuable part of the team, but Randy was the glue. He was the peacemaker, the encourager, and the one who pulled us together when anything threatened to pull us apart. He did it at work, at church, and in his family. What a blessing are the ones that bring unity.

chapter six

Applied F.I.T. Skills

What is the difference between a skill and an applied skill? Shouldn't every skill be applied? While it might seem obvious, many employees have skills that they do not apply consistently on a day-to-day basis on behalf of their employers. Like knowledge, a skill that is not applied is a skill that produces no productivity for the company and one that should not be rewarded.

Applied skills differ from technical skills in that they are skills that every employee can and should be able to develop and use, regardless of their job title or department. Applied skills work in the accounting office, the loading dock, the assembly line, and even in the CEO's office. An interesting aspect of applied skills is that the higher up you go in an organization, the more important applied skills become, quickly surpassing technical skill proficiency as an indicator of leadership success.

The Authority of Competency

Regardless of any employee's position or title, there are three specific and significant skills I wish every employee had. To have them may not make our lights brighter, but they burn dimmer if we don't have them. I call them F.I.T. skills. They involve the credibility factor, especially among our coworkers and our supervisors. They are:

- Follow-through
- Initiative
- Time-task reliability

Follow-Through Is the "F" in F.I.T.

The meaning of the term seems obvious. One fresh way to grasp it is to point to its opposite. These are excuses I've heard people give. It's unfortunate, but they're real. This doesn't mean just because they're real we have to say, "Well, I can't do this because . . . "

Changing Priorities

This is the first foe of follow-through.

The organizations we work for constantly shift directions and primary concerns. This is true of every company that wants to flourish and make profit in today's marketplace. What may have been a priority when they hired us may no longer be the same major objective today, tomorrow, or the month after that.

Instead of acknowledging and cooperating with this shift, too often we hear:

- "This is not the job I was hired for."
- "This isn't what I agreed to do when I started to work

here. I'm willing to do my job, but this *is not* part of
my job."
- "If they want to change, that's fine. Just get out of the
way and let me keep doing *my* job."

We've heard those excuses and others like them. Those
bright lights hit the dimmer switch hard when they insist on
business staying the way it used to be and refuse to adapt to
reality around them.

Haven't we all heard of the bookkeepers who wouldn't use
technology because "I've been doing it this way for thirty years
and my adding machine still works"? I know of companies that
had to fire typists because they refused to learn computer skills.

The world is changing, and this change is the one constant
we can expect. Today isn't like yesterday; what a company used
to do isn't good enough if they still want to be in business
tomorrow. These changes affect everyone. Our bosses constantly have to shift priorities according to factors that affect
their bosses, customers, and the marketplace.

The marketplace is in turmoil right now. I say *right now,*
because we've never had the rapidity of the change that has
been taking place in the marketplace that we've had in the last
twenty years.

Technology has expanded and continues to alter everything. Global competition has upset the old ways of doing
things. Regulation and deregulation have forced us to adopt
new methods. The labor force changes all the time. So do financial and economic factors, as well as customer opportunities

and problems, credits, profits, and opportunities. What company today can set seven-year plans in place and run with them and not be forced to make changes?

In short, the inconsistencies brought on by shifting priorities sometimes make it difficult to follow through. We may start walking down a path with clearly defined objectives, and we know where we're going. But guess what? Halfway down the path, the direction shifts, and we travel to a different location.

What can we say to people who are caught like that? I have only four words: *Get used to it!* That's normal. Business isn't going to stop changing. The only thing that won't change is the fact that things are changing.

As those committed to Unconditional Excellence, we not only need to accept change, but also to expect it. Even that's not enough. We need to prepare ourselves to adapt. Regardless of how much flux there is, *we* have to adjust. The best way to show that we acknowledge, accept, and adjust to altered priorities is that we follow through on whatever we're given to do.

Poor Planning
This is the second enemy of follow-through.

"I can't get it done because I don't have enough time," is an excuse we hear frequently—and most often from the same people. Behind the excuse is usually poor time management. (We'll talk more about that.)

Here's a personal example of what I mean by poor planning. Because of my position, I have to do what I call creative writing—setting down the innovative ideas that keep our corporation moving forward. When I get into my creative mode, I need peace and lack of disruption. How do I plan for that? The simplest way is for me to go into the conference room, close the door, and put up a sign:

> *Curmudgeon at Work.*
> *Don't Disturb until 11:00.*

Anyone who sees that sign will understand exactly what I mean. I *plan* not to be disturbed. This not-to-be-interrupted creative time works when I plan for it to work, and I have to be responsible to make it happen.

One day, about a month before I started on this book, I went into my office (not the conference room, which was my first mistake). I left my door open (my second mistake). I didn't hang a sign on my door (my third mistake). My assistant, Kevin, came to the door and said, "Hi, Alan? How's it going today?"

After I said the usual, "Fine," Kevin gave me a quick run-down on his weekend—something he often did. Then he went on to his office. Less than a minute later Rich came by, saw my door open, and said, "Hello, Alan," and we started talking. That conversation lasted about fifteen minutes before Rich walked away.

Then I paused and thought about what happened. Whose fault was it?

"They interrupted me," I could have said.

"They stopped and talked about unimportant things, and I couldn't be rude and ask them to go away," I might have wailed.

No, it was my fault because I didn't plan well. Earlier, I

listed all three mistakes I made. It was obvious that not only had I failed to follow through, but I had also not planned to succeed. I created the problem because my open door invited my coworkers inside.

I also realized that if I knew I would be interrupted—and common sense would have told me that I would be—I shouldn't plan to do high-concentration tasks that require completion in a short period of time. In most instances, the phone rings, or the receptionist buzzes me, or people in the office want to talk. My open door allows for all of that. Good planning for me means that I do three things: Attempt to balance the level of my work so that I decide on what I need to do; allow no one to divert me from the task; and then get it done.

Time Bandits

This is the third foe.

Most of us know that other people are the most notorious time bandits. They quietly steal our time. We have to watch this carefully because they may mean well. They seem to be everywhere, ready to grab three minutes or ten or maybe half an hour. We have to keep a constant vigil against them.

Sometimes *we ourselves* are the time bandits who hinder our own work. It's not so much failing to plan as an unconscious failing by not planning. It works like this. I've been at my desk ten minutes and I feel thirsty, so I stop at the watercooler for a drink. Mark is there and we talk about the football game, politics, new fashions, or our kids.

Perhaps worse, we spend twenty minutes together while

both of us lament over our workloads. "I'm so busy," I say, "I just can't possibly get everything done."

"Then don't go to the watering hole," someone might urge me.

"Yes, but relationship-building is important, too," I would then protest. "I can't be rude. I need to show Mark that I'm there for him and that I'm a coworker, and—"

"Yes, but you did it on company time," comes from a deep inner voice (if I'm honest with myself). "You didn't give your best and your first priority to your work."

Relationship building is certainly one of the issues each of us needs to face. How do we build and maintain good relationships and still get our work done? I have no easy answer. I do have to say that, although I'm a very relational person, doing the job I'm paid to do must be my first concern. That's why vigilance is so important. It's not an easy line to walk, but it's what we have to do to maintain Unconditional Excellence and to ward off the time thieves.

I've learned that some of the worst time bandits are coworkers—people I really like and enjoy being with. We need to identify them before we can strategize on how to stop them from stealing our time.

For example, I'll tell you about Paul, who held a high position in the J. Smith Lanier Company. We took the company leaders through the process of Unconditional Excellence that we called Beyond World Class[1]. When we reached the section on time bandits, we asked everyone, "Who are the time bandits in this group?"

[1]See *Beyond World Class: Building Character, Relationships, and Profit,* by Alan M. Ross with Cecil Murphey. (Chicago: Dearborn, 2002).

I meant it as a rhetorical question, but almost everyone pointed or shouted, "Paul."

A very surprised Paul blinked several times, looked around, and asked, "What do you mean?"

"At least once a day you go from cubicle to cubicle. You disrupt our work with small talk," one of them said.

"You never ask if it's convenient or if we're busy," said another. "You just go from one funny story to another and you keep the conversation going."

"That's right," said another. "You're the number-one time bandit." Although everybody chuckled, they knew that it was a bigger deal than Paul had thought it was. Paul the time bandit had stolen their productivity and performance.

Those words shocked, embarrassed, and upset Paul. He tried to explain that he was just being friendly—and everyone acknowledged they understood that.

We also learned later in one-to-one interviews that Paul was also the resident rumormonger. If there was any gossip in any department or about any individual, Paul knew it and was quite happy to pass it on to anyone willing to listen.

Intuitively, every individual in that room knew how Paul disrupted their work and spread rumors, but he was such a friendly person, and he did work hard—*when* he worked—that no one had previously acknowledged it.

We had to teach the others in the office to help Paul teach himself not to be the major time bandit. In various ways, each of them learned to stop him.

Paul's harshest response came from one man, who would

say, "I can't deal with time bandits right now."

Most of them weren't able to be that candid, but they put Paul in his place. More gently, another told him, "Let me get this finished. Then, if I can, I'll talk to you."

Months later I ran into Paul at a social occasion, and he let me know that things had changed at his company and he was no longer happy there. "I just tried to spread a little sunshine and make it a friendlier atmosphere," he said.

Wrong priority, is what I thought, but I didn't say it. I'm happy to say that the last I heard of Paul he had become far more productive and his coworkers appreciate his new sensitivity to their time.

Multitasking
This is the fourth enemy.

I refer to people who by natural temperament aren't concrete linear thinkers, even though their work may depend on their being able to complete a project before moving on to the next. Those people jump from one subject to another with ease, yet they display little ability to bring any job to completion. "She's always chasing one wild rabbit after another and rarely stays on one trail very long." The problem of most multitaskers isn't that severe, but this can be a troublesome area if we're not vigilant.

I'm not a natural linear thinker. I don't go from point A to B to C to D. I might start at R and jump to D before I hit A. That is to say that many of us aren't natural linear thinkers, but we can learn to develop that part of ourselves. Just as linear thinkers can jump into more right-brain activities, right-brain types can follow straight lines when they need to. We who call ourselves the creative types like to move in new directions and see possibilities ahead. When we're paid to do linear thinking and to demonstrate follow-through on that thinking, that's not the time to switch into our mode of random thinking.

We may find ourselves in jobs that demand serious linear thinking all day. If that's not our natural bent, we're probably miserable. For instance, if anyone made me an accountant—an extremely linear occupation—before two years were over, the IRS would probably put the CEO and other officials in prison because I wouldn't have finished half the things I'd been assigned to do. I would probably get a third of the way and then see something else that needed doing.

When confronted, I'd probably have to admit, "Oh, *that* government report? Yes, I knew about it, but I got a phone call . . . " I wouldn't finish the task, because I'm not very attentive to details about things I don't care about.

This means that if we're cast in the wrong role, we'll find that it's a constant problem with follow-through. My cowriter, Cec Murphey, once employed a woman named Judy. When she took the job, she said it was for more money than she'd ever made before. She had a bright smile and delightful disposition, but she constantly lagged behind in what she was supposed to do, and every week someone had to help her finish. Eventually, Judy admitted that she disliked the work and put off doing all the important things as long as possible. Cec fired her and then helped her find a job that was more suited to her temperament.

If like Judy we can't get the job done—assuming the

requirements are reasonable—we need to find the place where we can use and enjoy using our God-given skills and gifts.

Doing Only What We Like to Do

This is the fifth foe to follow-through.

I used to tell my employees, "You need to learn the difference between what you like to do and what you have to do. I'll help you find things you like to do. But I won't help you unless you finish the things you have to do *first*."

My experience has been that I find far too many Christian workers who fail to do what must be done because they are too busy doing what they *want* to do. Then they wonder why they are rebuked or terminated. Remember Nick, who was put on probation because he did what he wanted first.

Initiative Is the "I" in F.I.T.

I try to teach initiative to my employees as well as to my own children. One reason I'm sensitive is that I see so little true ingenuity on the job—from any employee, regardless of faith.

"If you give me a task, I'll do it," said one employee, flushed with obvious pride. "I won't let you down. Everything you ask me to do, I'll do."

That's good, but that's not initiative. As soon as someone asks us to do something beyond what we're currently doing, we may joyfully concur, but we've lost the initiative.

Here's how initiative works. First, we have an assigned job. If we don't follow through, that's not even being competent. Suppose Harriette came to me and said, "I've finished all the reports that were due today and made all the calls to remind the salespeople." Those are her assigned tasks. I'd say she was a good worker. That's still not initiative.

"I straightened out the file cabinet because I've noticed that it drives you nuts when you can't find the files you want. Oh, if you need me for anything else, I'll be in Evelyn's office. She's having trouble with her computer and she's gotten a little behind."

That's initiative.

To illustrate this, I want to tell you about Julie Falcone, the executive assistant to the CEO at the S. D. Myers Company. I cite Julie because she's the epitome of the word *initiative*. She does everything that she needs to do and follows through on everything. She doesn't stop with doing what she's supposed to do. She constantly discovers things that go beyond anything expected of her. She seeks ways to be helpful to coworkers and to serve the company better.

Her boss loves what she does.

I love it because I do a lot of work with S. D. Myers, and Julie Falcone helps me make it happen.

When I first began to work with S. D. Myers, I have to admit that some of the other leaders expressed resentment toward Julie and her resourcefulness. Why didn't they like it? Because when Julie took initiative, they felt it made them look bad (it did) and that she kept things humming when they could easily have done some of those jobs themselves (and they probably should have).

Julie doesn't take over or push anyone aside. She does her

work as part of her commitment to Unconditional Excellence. When she has finished her work, she is not one to sit by and do nothing. Almost everyone told me that she'd walk over to the other departments and ask, "Is there anything I can do to help?" or "Let's get this done. I can work with you and we'll finish it off in an hour."

Here's the problem she faced. By taking initiative she also stirred up resentment.

Julie wanted to be Unconditionally Excellent and to be resourceful, but she didn't want to stir up resentment. Here's an example of what she did. She went directly to the head of the human resources (HR) department, for instance, and said, "Here's what I think we could work on together. What do you think? Can you use my help?"

She allowed the head of HR to take the credit for her initiative—Julie didn't care who got credit. Within a short time she had no lack of people wanting her help and begging her to assist them. The resentment had evaporated.

Julie understood a subtle thing. If we take initiative and at the same time need people to notice or praise us, we have violated the humility factor. There's also another, more subtle factor here. If we take initiative and make sure we get credit, we usually go on and take the next step. We turn that initiative into political favor. That is, we seek to gain political favor.

Worse, once we move forward in power, we begin to hide the things we don't follow through on. We blame others for our failures, and we make sure we get seen as being indispensable.

Initiative is such a powerful tool that every leader yearns to see it in employees. It's also such a powerful tool that it has a huge potential for misuse politically.

Whenever I see people taking initiative, the first thing I ask their leader is, "Is she doing the things that you've asked her to do?" If the leader says no, I sit down with the employee and say, "Everyone loves your ingenuity, but . . . "

The second thing I look for and ask questions about is this: Is she doing it to the detriment of somebody else? Is she building somebody up, or is she saying, "I did this because Rhonda is incompetent or incapable."

When I perceive that attitude, I realize that I have a political animal on my hands. I need to be careful because if I feed that creature, eventually that animal will grow larger and come back and bite me.

There's nothing to prevent that animal from going to my boss and saying, "Well, I suppose you know that Alan didn't get this report done quite right. He's a nice, friendly man, and I like him a lot. In fact, I used to look up to him as the best employee in the place. But he's—well, he's changed recently. He's just not pulling his weight. But don't worry. I've taken care of this report for you, and I'll make sure you get what you need." Then the animal sighs and says, "But some days I just get a little tired of covering up for him."

There's another problem that comes from walking the fine line of initiative; those with initiative must be able to see a need for themselves, without a superior pointing it out. They need to be willing to do those above-and-beyond tasks, *but also they need to be a team player.*

When I spot independent, initiating types, a question pops into my mind: Are they also capable of being *interdependent*? Good business procedures need the concept of "We do this together." When anyone consistently takes on a Lone Ranger role, that person actually harms the working environment, even if he or she works three times as hard as anyone else does.

If a person with initiative can function in an interdependent, team-working environment, we have an invaluable team player. In fact, that's the kind of person I look for.

Here's something else I've learned: It takes only one person with initiative to help a team reach higher performance levels. This is especially true if those initiators are willing to give credit to the team (or whoever they work with). In a team environment, not everyone needs initiative, but if no one has it, the work suffers.

Time-Task Reliability Is the "T" in F.I.T.

"I'll be there by 8:30," she says before she hangs up the phone. If she says it, I want to know that she'll be there no later than 8:30. In fact, I take her statement as a promise.

Does that sound petty? It's far from a petty issue. In fact, it's absolutely critical in the workplace. The catchword we used to hear was "The currency of the '90s is money." In this century, the currency is *time*, because money is no longer the central concern.

"I just don't have enough time to . . . " I probably hear that five times every day. I've even said it myself.

It irks me when the people who complain about not having enough time habitually walk in at 8:35 or even 8:50. They know that office hours begin at 8:30, and that's also when their paid time begins.

Do they then go to their desks and rush into the things that require immediate attention? Of course not. They have to get their morning coffee, say hello to their coworkers, and update everyone on the previous night's activities. They probably also answer personal e-mail before they settle down to their jobs.

They steal their first hour from the company that pays their salary. They're not only stealing time—but if time is the currency of this decade, they have stolen the most valuable currency of all. They also tend to be the first to complain that they don't have enough time to "follow through" on the tasks that are assigned to them, and most certainly they can't show initiative if they don't have the time.

As those who advocate Unconditional Excellence, we must put the faithful use of our time high on our list. How can we be excellent if we squander, ignore, or steal this precious commodity from our employers?

This isn't a book about time management. My purpose here is to urge readers to ask themselves this question: "How do I develop a workable system of time management?"

I thought for quite a while about that question before I finally turned it upside down. *How do I make all my work time devoted time?*

"Devoted time? Devoted to what?" someone asked me.

Here's how I answer. Suppose I start every day with an affirmation to be excellent. How do I bring that about? I can do it when I arrive on time and start my workday with a simple prayer: *God, use me today. Let my hours be devoted to modeling your excellence.* I can attest to the power of this concept, and so can others who have focused on it.

Once we've set the example of faithfully using devoted time, people may ask, "How do you do it? You seem to get so much done and yet you're calm and at peace, even in the midst of the chaos going on around here. How do you do that?"

I like to think of devoted time as "while I . . . then I" time. Here are examples:

- While I am working with a team . . . then I will apply my excellent communications skills to that team.
- While I am completing this task . . . then I will make sure I use my abilities to be creative, innovative, and to demonstrate follow-through to the end.
- While I lead all of the employees entrusted to me . . . then I will teach, mentor, and challenge them to set a level of Unconditional Excellence in their own lives and to let it become their personal standard. I will leave a legacy.

Because we live with the tyranny of the urgent, our good use of time—the currency of the millennium—provides a valuable model to people desperately seeking answers. They may not say it, but what their attitude implies is: "Hmm, okay, I'm going to watch to see how excellent you are with your time." This is one of the biggest tests of being Unconditionally Excellent. If we model the best, we also create a model that others want to emulate.

Time and Personal Destiny

Let's revisit this whole concept of personal destiny again as it relates to time. I'm going to make a bold declaration.

Those who are truly contented with where they are on their path to personal destiny are not in a constant hurry.

The greatest regret I have about my own career isn't that I didn't accomplish more; I regret that I didn't slow down and enjoy more of the journey. I have spent most of my life, even my precareer life, in a "When I . . . then I" mode of operations.

- When I get the raise . . . then I will spend more time with the kids.
- When I get the promotion . . . then I will be able to slow down.
- When I finish this book . . . then I will take the family skiing.

This attitude becomes part of our makeup. Ambition is a good thing, but it is also potentially destructive. Ambition can keep us rushing, always rushing, to the next goal and the one after that and those over the next horizon. We can do much for ourselves if we pause to reflect on this question: *What am I putting off until I finish my current "when I . . . "?*

If we can truly make the transformation from "When I . . ."

to "While I . . ." we will be able to move beyond being constantly frustrated doing our best right now—and doing it with excellence. We learn to move at a healthier, wiser pace.

I love the word *pace*. I believe every person, every team, and every business has a unique pace. When we push too hard against our natural speed or we slow down and pull against it, we lose the ease with which our pace can move us along.

By contrast, Jesus called for those of us who are weary to take his yoke upon ourselves. That sounds like even more work, but then he said his yoke was well fitting (sometimes translated as *easy*) and his burden light. He used metaphorical language, in which the idea of taking on a yoke is a symbol of submission. When we submit to the divine leadership that leads us to excellence, our tasks are those suited to our personalities. What might otherwise seem boring, difficult, and frustrating becomes easy and enjoyable.

One of the things that makes the yoke around my neck painful and frustrating is that I push against the natural pace that God created for me. When I find my speed and flow with it, an amazing peace and sense of purposeful direction come over me. That is part of what makes us Unconditionally Excellent.

chapter seven

The Skill to Create and Innovate

"I just never think of things like that."

"He's always coming up with new ideas, but I never seem to have any original ideas."

"She's creative, and I'm not."

How many of us have heard those words? How many of us have said those words or words like them? Many of us don't consider ourselves creative, and yet we may be better at it than we're aware.

Original Creativity

I distinguish between original and synthetic creativity. Literally, no one is originally creative; that is God's domain. Yet we use those things that God has provided. Someone developed silicon out of sand and then went on to conceive of the silicon chip. God gave us the sand, the mind, and the capacity to invent such things. From the silicon chip came computers, and from computers came the restructuring and changing of the modern world.

Some of us are predisposed to original ideas. For such people, this is a gift—it's something truly God-given. I like to think of it as God passing on that ingenious ability to humanity. Certainly, it's not something we can teach.

Too many people came through a school system that insisted, "There is only one answer to every question." That's linear learning. It prevents a high level of independent thinking. It's what I call living in the accounting mode. This is linear, logical thinking that insists that from step A we can only go to step B and then only to C.

I don't mean to criticize or imply that analytic types are of less value to an organization. They are immeasurably valuable, especially in areas of follow-through, initiative, and reliability. I also know that analytical people can learn and succeed in the second creative area, what I call synthetic creativity.

My concern is that in some instances, our culture teaches us to respond to situations around us in a linear fashion. As a result, we categorize those who don't conform as eccentric or strange.

Smitty is a dear friend and a former employee. I fired him twenty years ago because he couldn't follow through or stay focused on his task. He disrupted any office we put him in because he was just too funny for other people to work around. He never knew when to turn off the humor.

Smitty later became a history teacher in high school. The kids love him because he makes history memorable and fun and because his presentation is humorous. Smitty finally found his niche. He's using his original creativity and his love for history to make a difference. He won't get rich as a teacher, but his personal destiny has become clear and he is using his God-given gift in a remarkable way.

Three Examples of Original Creativity

Original creativity tends to look at a situation and turn it on its side or on its head. I want to cite three examples.

First, my cowriter teaches and often produces articles on writing. An editor wanted him to write about literary agents. The most obvious question for most aspiring writers is, "How do I get an agent?" That was the question his article was supposed to answer. Instead of starting with the question (step A), he started with something more like step Q. He tapped into that creative part of himself and called his article, "Why Would an Agent Want to Represent Me?" He provided the same information, but he turned the question around for writers to examine themselves.

Because of his clever way of responding, that article has been published and republished. It has been included in books on writing, and many consider it a classic on the topic. Cec Murphey didn't know any more about agents than anyone else, and he didn't spend five years researching. He simply took an imaginative approach to answering a common question.

Second, here's an illustration from my experience. Shortly after I became the head of Sklar Peppler, a furniture company in Canada, I had to make a presentation to my board of directors. I was supposed to meet with them for a breakfast meeting at 7:00 the next morning and explain my "restructuring strategy for a very sick company."

I didn't have a strategy. I knew all of the problems. I just wasn't certain of the solutions.

For days I had worked at my presentation, but nothing came to me. I wadded up and threw away dozens of pages from my yellow legal pad. I paced, I groaned, I prayed, I relaxed, and I also pushed myself hard. Still nothing. I skimmed through a dozen books, and re-examined all my management skills. I tried every approach I knew and nothing felt right.

The size and scope of this problem was beyond my experience. Every time I came up with an idea or a strategy, it soon paled in comparison to the magnitude of the problems.

When I went to bed at 11:00 P.M. I still didn't have a solution. Surprisingly, I was at peace. I had no idea what I would say the next morning, but as I lay in bed, I prayed for God's help. "Lord, I need your wisdom on this. I need to see this situation the way you see it."

I must have prayed in that vein for a couple of minutes. I drifted off to sleep and slept soundly. At 6:00 the next morning, I awakened and felt absolutely refreshed. During the night I wasn't aware of dreaming, and I didn't wake up with a divine revelation surging through my brain. I felt as if the clouds of confusion had lifted. It was as if I had been walking around on a humid, foggy day. Immediately, the sun shone, the skies were blue, and the grass had turned a brilliant green.

The clarity of my thoughts was unbelievable. With less than an hour before my meeting, I knew exactly what to do. I sat down and wrote a turnaround strategy, complete with time lines and staffing requirements. I sketched out a management team structure. As I wrote it, I realized that it was a highly creative approach to a very significant problem in the company.

It was also exactly on target. After I presented my idea, the chairman of the board nodded in agreement and said, "That sounds like he has the plan. Let's do it." Then he walked out of the room. My plan took more than three years to complete, but the plan we executed over the whole course of that company turnaround was my original idea—and it worked.

My ideas, which aren't important enough to spell out, were not in any textbook I had ever read or from any lecture I'd heard at college or picked up from a seminar guru. I don't want to sound like some kind of mystic seer. I'm not that. I'm a highly pragmatic business leader.

So what happened?

People without faith would likely say that I just came up with it. I didn't. I emptied my head of everything. I started with a clean mental sheet of paper and a good night's sleep. When I awakened, the entire plan was there, full-blown. That is one of the major ingredients to original creativity—the willingness to start with nothing and wait for the answer.

Here's my third example. Jack McGeadey was vice president of sales and marketing for Ochs Industries. Ochs called in our organization, Corporate Development Institute (CDI), to help them with their sales-and-marketing strategy, design, and engineering. Essentially, Ochs Industries manufactured the metal housings for some of the best technology companies in the world, such as Intel, Compaq, Dell, and Hewlett Packard.

Ochs Industries worked with those companies' engineering teams, designing the housing to make their products better, faster, stronger, and cheaper. They had a great design and engineering team, probably one of the best in the world. In fact, the imaginative engineers and product development people at Intel came to depend on Ochs as much for this ability as they did for their ability to manufacture the housings.

Metal housings in computers certainly aren't as sexy a part of the computer as electronics or chips. The plastics can be the pretty part, but the metal is the foundational structure— although not attractive, the metal part is extremely important in electromagnetic environments.

After the technology slump of the late 1990s, orders for housings dropped to an all-time low. The manufacturing plants were either not working or barely operational. In fact, the slump got so severe that the future of the fifty-year-old company was in question.

Jack refused to give in. He was already receiving many requests for his Ochs design and engineering experts to begin work on the next generation of technology products. Industry leaders knew that when the slump was over, their customers were going to buy the best and the newest products, bypassing those carried over from the past few years. Research and development worked intensely at companies such as Intel to be ready for the business turnaround.

Without knowing when or if a product order would come, Jack met with his design people and sought innovative ways to support Intel. After Jack and I had visited a number of his customers, I challenged him. "Look at your customers' needs now, in light of this slump. Obviously, they don't need manufacturing. What do they need?"

Jack came back with the answer. He and the Ochs designers put their collective heads together and came up with an outstanding idea that he called "design service." "We can sell that service," he said to his people. They used design service to begin a new division. I knew Jack well and he was a bright light in a dark world, as well as a deeply committed man of faith.

"Where did you come up with that idea?" I asked him.

"I was sitting in Intel's office in Seattle and we were talking with several executives. They kept referring to the work done by our two design engineers. More than once, they said, 'You guys know this better than we do, and it's our product.'

"I listened, but the first time it didn't get through to me. The second time they said something like that, I thought, that's true. Our people do know more about the design than you do. Then I took that thought a little further. Our people know more and yet you're quibbling over money with us on the cost of the boxes, trying to shave off a bit here and there. I also realized that it would have been cheaper for Intel if they went to China and had the boxes made there. If they did that, we couldn't have competed with their cheap labor. I also realized they stayed with us because they wanted our design engineers. They saw that when they presented us with a problem, we solved it quickly, cheaply, and easily."

Jack smiled and said, "Then we decided that if we could do a good job for Intel, we could do just as good a job for anyone else."

Ochs Industries established a new division called Ochs Solutions and said to the various corporations, "We would like to solve your problems by letting you buy our design services. Once you've done that you can shop anywhere in the world to have it put together. In fact, we'll design it for high volume in China or for lower runs here in the United States. Rather than our trying to design it for us to make, we'll design everything so that you can take it wherever you want and get it produced as cost effectively as possible."

At first, Intel didn't like the idea of paying for something they'd previously gotten for free. They finally agreed. Once they started using Ochs Solutions, they understood they had an extremely valuable ally for their product. Ochs Industries soon became the pre-eminent design and engineering firm for the metal boxes that all of those electronics fit inside.

At the time of this writing, most Ochs Industries plants are idle. Because of the slump in the high-tech industry, their sales fell from close to a $100 million to about $10 million. The only cash-positive, fast-growing contribution to the business—and the one thing that will probably help them survive—is Ochs Solutions, which their vice president of sales and marketing, Jack McGeadey, dreamed up. That's creativity at work.

Design and engineering always precede any emergence from a recession. As the electronics industry goes through its ups and downs, guess who's *not* going to go through the ups and downs with them? It's the design and engineering phase of this higher-margin, low-capital, and very solutions-intensive service. Creativity in its original sense comes there.

Synthetic Creativity

Synthetic creativity is the ability to take things that have already been invented or developed and find new, previously untried uses for them. It's the ability to say, "Somebody solved the filing problem in client services. If I took that same approach and applied it to customer service, or if I applied that solution in manufacturing, you know what? We could save ourselves a lot of time and energy."

I've discovered that there are more synthetically imaginative people than originally creative ones. It's not a gift or innate ability; it's a skill that we can teach, so that people can take ideas and products and improve on them.

It works like this. We begin with the solution in mind. We ask, "What do we want to accomplish?" or "Where do we want to end up?"

Then we examine our situation. We ask what would happen if our:

- Customer services were working right?
- Telephone system, e-mail system, and entire communication system functioned efficiently?
- Paper-flow systems improved dramatically?
- Accounting systems functioned without glitches?
- Information systems operated at peak?

Once we ask such questions, we go back to that solution and begin to seek imaginative applications. Some might call it adaptation. In reality, a lot of our suppliers and customers have done that. People in different areas of a corporation become aware of the original design; after that, it takes only one skilled person to say, "We could adapt that to fit our situation."

I see this applied a great deal in the information technology (IT) world. For example, many companies find reliable software. They get people to adjust it and then they do whatever it takes to make it function for their organization. There's a huge win for companies that value synthetic creativity. They realize that most of the beta work has already been done. When software is first developed, the beta customers are the first to run it, debug it, and suggest recommended changes, yet even after those changes are made, the software must be applied to each specific customer's unique circumstances. While the beta testing and development process creates a better, more reliable product, it is the ability to make that product work specifically to meet our needs that defines synthetic creativity.

We try to teach people that when they see programs or procedures that work in an organization or in a different department, they should ask, "Can this work for us?"

Too often we get the opposite response. We know what others have done. Instead of admiring and adapting, we resent it that someone else came up with the solution. Therefore, we don't investigate. It's so much better if we ask, "How can we use that service or product here? How can we take what the manager did in sales and marketing and apply it in our division?"

When we apply synthetic creativity, we tend to want to make it seem more difficult than it is for fear that we won't get the credit. There is no greater way to stimulate coworkers than to recognize their contribution to our creative solution. In companies, it builds an innovative culture where the best ideas and solutions are shared openly. It generates win-win solutions.

We also recognize that when we work synthetically, we have to make adjustments. Our situations are different, and so are our people. Even our customers are different. We can still take the wheel that someone invented, adjust the size, and put it on our own vehicle.

I want to go back to what I said at the beginning of this section. Ingenuity works if we start with the end result in mind. "What do I want to see happen?" Once we know the solution we desire, we evaluate what's already out there in the marketplace. As we examine each product or plan, we ask, "Will it provide what I want?"

We'll discover that synthetic creativity will produce most of what we want, although there will be gaps that we must fill in. It's simply a gap analysis when we go back and ask, "What do I have to change about that solution to make it fit our situation?"

Typically, we adjust. We fill in gaps to create the solution that fits our needs. It functions best when we're talking about teaming because, frankly, most things have been done before. We then ask, "How did that team solve the problem? What systems did they use to do that?" If we're open-minded, we might discover that what they figured out, we can use. Because it's a different problem and a different team, we may also come up with new ideas or even improve on it. That's synthetic creativity.

Innovation

Innovation refers to the ability to apply either original or synthetic creativity to improve what we want or to increase performance or productivity.

Here's the sad news. All too often, those who are the most original and inspired are incapable of innovation. They can come up with brilliant solutions but then they stop. It's as if they are standing at the end of the road and can see nothing ahead. They simply can't see the roads to their left or right.

From my experience, I've learned that the makeup of a team includes a source of creative solutions. For some team purposes there is a greater need for original creativity, and others need those who can apply those amazing insights. The size and scope of the task and the available resources help determine the type of skill needed on the team. I also want to include an innovator on the team. Without that quality present, the team may come up with many great, ingenious solutions, but it will never figure out how to make the solutions work practically, quickly, and with the least amount of disruption.

Perhaps it helps to show the difference between the original thinkers and the applied thinkers this way. The creative say, "This is what we could do." The innovative say, "And this is how we'll use it."

There's one other significant factor here. Innovators are the pragmatists. They look ahead and anticipate the problems that creativity brings. They're the first ones to say, "And if that happens, then we can . . . " They are solutions providers by virtue of their ability to see beyond immediate needs and problems.

Too many organizations fail, not because they're not originally or synthetically creative, but because they don't know how to innovate—that is, they don't know how to apply what is offered to them.

If it comes to a choice, I'd say that we're going to be further along the way toward Unconditional Excellence if we have great innovations and limited creativity than if we have the reverse. The ideal, obviously, is to have both working together harmoniously. When that happens, we're Unconditionally Excellent, and we blow away the competition.

For example, years ago I worked as a senior consultant with a company called Team Resources. Pat MacMillan, the founder of Team Resources, is one of the most synthetically insightful people I have ever met. He is able to grasp loose ends as opportunities rather than problems.

One of our client companies was Construction Market Data (CMD). Today they are the largest and best provider of construction information to the supply industry, but before they worked with Team Resources, hardly anyone had heard of them.

While CMD was serving regional customers well, whenever they met a competitive situation with a national customer, they lost out to their rivals. Though CMD had better information, better systems, and better prices, they couldn't meet the needs of the national customers.

Because CMD's founder, Errol Woffords, welcomed Pat MacMillan's ability to innovate, Pat produced a brilliant solution for CMD to become a national player in the construction market information industry. While Errol knew where he wanted to go, he had assumed it would take slow and deliberate growth, such as adding regional offices and staff to fill in all of the gaps before they became a national company.

Essentially, all CMD provides to a customer is information. For the Carrier Corporation, a provider of air conditioning systems, to be successful, they need advance information for their sales force to know where and when construction projects are being planned. CMD and others provide that information. A regional supplier of lumber products might be happy with regional information, but a company like Carrier must have national, and eventually international, construction market information.

Pat challenged the thinking that to be a national company they had to have a national presence. He presented a creative solution that other industries were already applying.

I realized CMD had an incredible team of dedicated leaders with many different skills and abilities. Once the national project went from potential, using synthetically created solutions, to plan, it took a great deal of innovative thinking to overcome all of the obstacles and pitfalls.

First, the sales and marketing staff had to develop an innovative way to approach the market. They did.

Second, the technology staff had to solve a myriad of interface problems. They did.

Third, the human resources staff had to develop a rapid-growth-and-training plan to support the launch. They did.

CMD involved every aspect of the business in the innovative implementation. Within one year—a full four years sooner than they had thought possible, and certainly far sooner than their competition had planned for—CMD went to their trade show and hit a home run. The runs keep coming, and the wins keep piling up.

The Age of Enlightenment

We have many problems in the world today. Solving those problems will take all the imagination and innovation we have available. Through God we have access to unlimited creativity. We need to be more open to new ways of thinking and be able to adapt others' solutions to solve some of these problems. We can't accomplish that by continuing to do what we have always done.

It's much like the fly trying to get out of the house by constantly banging against the same window. We need to find new doors and new avenues of escape.

At the time Christ walked the earth, Roman rule, or *Pax Romana* (literally, the term means "Roman peace"), allowed the Gospel to be spread to the ends of the earth. Today the new rule is *Pax Capitala,* or the rule of free market economics and free enterprise. Even communist China subscribes to it. Because of *Pax Capitala*, we can use the system of free enterprise to generate enormous wealth for a select few. Alternatively, we can use this opportunity to make Unconditional Excellence a major component of the solution to very complex problems.

I have watched a unique phenomenon grow over the past twenty years, particularly over the last decade. I come across more and more people in business—men and women, black and white, Jewish and Christian, leaders and followers—who have decided that they want to make a difference through their careers. One of the things I take great delight in is that I expect (not permit, mind you) my employees to spend a considerable amount of their time applying their God-given skills in some sort of activity not related to work.

Earlier in the book I mentioned Ultimate Support Systems and the way Jim Dismore has made a difference in his community and in the lives of his employees. Unconditional Excellence functions best when we focus on others, especially those who need help.

Whether at their church, in their community, or on a short-term mission trip in a foreign country, I want employees to use their skills, particularly those of creativity and innovation, to serve others. Service has become a major part of each of our personal destinies that makes work that much more meaningful.

chapter eight

The Art of Solving Problems

"I want to keep Bob in my region," I said, "because he's the best rep I have at solving problems. The guy's a gem and if I lose him, not even two acceptable reps would be able to replace him."

We were in a manager's meeting discussing territory restructuring. Bob was a great sales rep, but more than that, he had an uncanny ability to recognize, analyze, and recommend solutions. Most of the difficulties he helped resolve impacted all the other sales reps, so his value was just as high to the other managers as it was to me.

"Everyone wants Bob," said Ron Spendley from the western region.

"Before you got here, Jimmy Jones tried to trade two reps now and a rep to be named later for him," joked Terry Martinez, the manager responsible for bringing both Bob and me into the company.

What is the point of this vignette? Those with the ability and willingness to solve issues are a treasure to any leader. If we put all of the skills in this book to use, yet we don't become adept at recognizing, analyzing, and resolving differences, we can still be good workers. If we can add this important skill, we will have attained Unconditional Excellence. Leaders sponsor, promote, treasure, and, yes, even drool over such invaluable assets because those who can create solutions are a manager's personal joy.

A Matter of Motivation

I can't emphasize this point strongly enough. Every skill we develop on our journey toward Unconditional Excellence takes us closer to becoming the most valuable, sought-after, and secure person in our organization. When we regularly use our skills to untangle difficulties, we become not only the best, but also the most wanted team member. I have seen businesses transformed, exploding with success and productivity when unconditional skills were applied to the solution of core issues. Not everyone can or will be able to settle difficulties, but those who figure out the breakthrough answers develop a confidence and presence that propels them in their career (opportunity for growth), makes their work more meaningful and fulfilling (meaningful work), creates a sense of unity and participation in the workplace (community), and increases pay benefits and job security to boot.

The things that we want from our careers are a direct result of our ability to be problem solvers, especially when we apply Unconditionally Excellent skills.

In the beginning of this book I wrote: If I told you I had a secret formula that would guarantee a successful career, what would you pay to get it? Here it is.

The Secret

At every level within organizations, those who see, analyze, and solve problems provide the greatest Return on Benefit Investment (ROBI) for their employers. Those employees will be given greater opportunities, be paid better, receive larger benefits, and enjoy significantly more career satisfaction than others.

If you're skeptical, ask any senior leader in any organization how valuable they find their direct reports—from administrative assistants to shop floor welders to truck drivers—when they become problem solvers.

I know what their response would be. I know what mine is.

Here's something else: Solving problems is a teachable skill, not an unteachable art. While there are people who are more adept or gifted at figuring out answers, there are approaches that anyone can apply. The biblical approach assumes that each of us has different gifts, skills, and temperaments; a one-size-fits-all approach therefore won't be biblical, and it probably won't work. Now let's look at how we learn to problem solve.

The Evolution of a Problem

Like simple, one-celled organisms, most troubles come to life when fed on just one thing. Problems are usually caused, or fed, by circumstances. When we change the way we operate, alter the conditions, or make almost any type of business-related decision, we give birth to trouble. Since problems usually start small, they are often as hard to detect as a single cell in a petri dish. As various conditions evolve and change the environment, the issue grows. It spins off new cells—what I call symptom cells. The new cells may look like the problem, or they may look entirely different. Most employees are able to see the symptoms clearly.

As adverse situations increase, the symptom cells multiply, and we have to deal with a nasty little crisis that now looks like a petri dish festering with primordial ooze. Symptom cells are potentially poisonous, often deadly, and they almost always join with other cells. Symptoms and situations feed off each other; often, it is difficult to know when one begins and another ends.

We spend most of our time dealing with these symptom cells and circumstances while the trouble itself remains masked.

Another illustration I like is that of an organ grinder with what appears to be a cute, lovable little monkey. That's where troubles start. If not dealt with, that tiny little creature evolves into a larger, more aggressive primate. After a few more feedings, it becomes a gigantic, angry, caged gorilla. We hand the animal a few peanuts, and he grabs our hands and mauls us. I've fed such animals and been mauled by gorillas. I imagine every leader out there has experienced the same. Any staff member who can help me avoid gorillas in the future will become my new friend and potential superhero.

The first step toward successfully solving difficulties is to learn to see obstructions from a different perspective. Initially, this is extremely difficult for most people. I tell them, "It's like learning to ride a bike—once you get it, you've got it for life."

By contrast, in any organization, almost everyone spots symptoms and they can explain them. Most employees see it as their right to tell their bosses about the blood on the gorilla's paw. Most of the time they don't recognize that the situation requires far more of them than just pointing out evidence of something wrong. They can't distinguish between symptoms, circumstances, and true crisis.

Problem solvers, however, have developed an obstruction-recognition perspective that allows them to wade through the circumstances, cut through the symptoms, and directly confront the core issue itself. Often, the magnitude of the symptoms and the noise from the circumstances surrounding the situation make it difficult to get through to the source. As the old saying tells us, we have to keep peeling away each layer on the onion until we get to the core. It may smell bad while we're doing this task, and at times we all want to scream or resign, but we keep going. Once we reach the core of any situation, we know what we are dealing with.

An illustration will help clarify the difference between problems, symptoms, and circumstances.

"We have a bad situation—really bad—and we'd like your help," were the first words Bob said to me on the phone. "We thought we had a handle on it, but for some reason the situation is getting worse." Bob was a good friend and former client. Several years before that call, I had taken Acme's executive leadership team through a planning and development process.

"Tell me what you think is the crisis, and I'll see if I think we can help," I answered.

"It's the plant in Houston. We just can't seem to make the productivity breakthrough we need. We have enough business to fill it up, but we're having a challenge keeping good workers. Turnover is too high; absenteeism and tardiness are at twice the rate of our Cleveland facility. It could be that we have a different culture down there, but I don't think so. We're getting our lunch eaten due to poor productivity." Bob was an engineer and fairly analytical. I was surprised that they had not been able to provide their own solution.

"That's not really what we do, you know," I said, "but I'll be glad to do a quick review and see what I would recommend in the way of a fix. I'd like to start at your plant in Cleveland and then go down to Houston."

"I'm not sure why you need to come up here, but I'm okay with it if it will solve our crisis."

I wanted to start in Cleveland because I suspected they had not gotten past the level of dealing with their symptoms—things that Bob had mentioned, like absenteeism, high employee turnover, and tardiness. These tend to be symptomatic of larger, hidden issues.

Here's a good statement of common sense: *Employees tend to send symptomatic signals when they are trying to get attention.* Rather than go through all the surrounding circumstances at Acme, I'll fast-forward to the issue we discovered. The vice president of human resources in Ohio had responsibility for both plants. She had several support people working for her in Texas, and for the most part they implemented the same policies and procedures that were implemented in Ohio.

The HR staff had good data on the extent of the situation. Employee turnover in Cleveland was 13 percent annually, which was good given the industry and their tight labor market. The Houston plant had an annual turnover rate of 29 percent, yet the labor market there was not as tight as it was in Cleveland. Additionally, every measure of employee time/task reliability was at least twice as bad in Texas as it was in Ohio. Absenteeism was almost three times higher than it was in Ohio.

All these issues combined to create a disastrous situation. They were losing a good bit of money. Even more alarming, they had made additional commitments to customers that would make the situation worse when those new commitments became orders.

Six months before Bob's call to me, the vice president of human resources had gotten together with both the Ohio and Texas production leadership. They discovered what they thought was the problem: Houston had never instituted the same point system that was used in Cleveland, where employees were assigned points for lateness, absenteeism, and for most disciplinary actions.

The Cleveland plant had been in operation for almost fifty years, and the point system was one of those management tools they were deeply committed to. The Houston operation was only a few years old. There, management felt the system was too cumbersome. They believed it took responsibility for control away from plant leadership and put it into the hands of the people in HR.

They decided to implement the point system in Texas, believing that the trouble was caused by a lack of control procedures. Within months of implementing the system, the difficulties increased and badly affected the morale of the line supervisors in the plant. They felt they had lost the trust of upper management and now had to take on the added burden of implementing a point system they didn't believe in.

After spending less than half a day with several of the line supervisors and several of the more productive employees in Houston, I flew back to Cleveland and met with the CEO.

"You don't have a time/task reliability crisis," I told Bob. "In fact, you never had one. You have a serous leadership and trust issue. Do you realize that the operations manager down there is the most dictatorial and unforgiving manager you have on the Acme payroll? He keeps the place in turmoil. The symptoms show up as absenteeism, tardiness, and turnover."

"Really? We considered him the best production manager around, and he came highly recommended by everyone we talked with."

"I'm sure he would do well in some environments but not at Acme. Your entire HR philosophy has been to hire good workers, pay them well, and honor them as valuable partners in your company. Your dad made it a hallmark of your company. In Houston, they hear that Acme cares—yes, they hear it, but they feel they're not treated as if the company cares."

"Why didn't the folks in HR catch it?" he asked.

"Maybe it was because they were too focused on the symptoms to look deep into the source. The leadership group was committed to their solution, which was institution of the point system, so I'm not sure they could have perceived anything beyond what they wanted to see. It wouldn't surprise me to find out that your manager in Texas had difficulties like this everywhere he has been."

Within three months, Bob hired a new manager, scrapped the point system, and made it a personal responsibility to be in Texas to make sure that the leaders adhered to the Acme policy of valuing employees.

Guess what happened? Productivity improved. Every time/task reliability measure dramatically improved, equaling or bettering the Ohio ratios. As a result, they began making a significant profit.

This is only one of hundreds of examples I could have cited to illustrate one of the most common factors of problem solving: We often focus on what we see as obviously wrong and don't get down to the source. In fact, if we "fix" a symptom, the predicament may actually get worse. Alternately, we can fix the immediate crisis. The symptom will go away, but the core issue will remain. While the Acme situation was a relatively large-scale dilemma, it illustrates a situation common to those every organization faces.

Separating Circumstances

We need to separate conditions, or circumstances, from symptoms and problems. Circumstances can create problems, make them worse, or mask them so they are even more difficult to uncover. Think of it this way: Conditions are incubators for crisis and the symptoms of crisis. That means we can alter conditions to eliminate symptoms and difficulties. Separating circumstances from the other two, however, takes practice and patience.

Let's visit the Acme situation once again.

- *The problem* was an abusive and misaligned leader.
- *The symptoms* were absenteeism, tardiness, and high employee turnover.
- What were *the circumstances* that fed them?

First: Rapid Growth

This caused hiring decisions at the leadership level that would have been handled differently had the pace of change not been so rapid. I have seen rapid growth create a huge array of difficulties and offshoot symptoms. Rapid growth not only causes difficulties, it also feeds and masks them. The obstacle isn't rapid growth—that's a symptom. There are businesses that grow rapidly, but they take time to anticipate and deal with the foreseeable crises before they threaten that growth.

Second: A "Silo Mentality"

In Acme's case, a silo mentality existed between human resources and plant operations. It actually fed the difficulties by trying to fix the symptoms. By "silo mentality," I mean a situation in which both departments act separately from the other in their own enclosed worlds. Silos are everywhere in business. I have made a good living fixing the chaos caused, fed, or hidden by silos. In management, the silo mentality also makes dealing with problems that much tougher: Typically, at least one of the silos has a vested and selfish interest in maintaining the status quo.

Finally: A New Plant

Conducting business with a plant located some distance from the home office was a circumstance that Acme had not previously encountered. For most organizations that's not an issue, but for a family-owned business with a fifty-year culture in Ohio, the distance itself fed the crisis. They would have detected the problems more quickly if they had taken place in Cleveland.

Once we become adept at identifying symptoms and circumstances, it becomes easier to perceive and solve the difficulties. In many cases, merely *seeing* the core issue solves the dilemma.

The Problem Scale

How do we develop this problem-perspective ability? Each of us has been equipped to do it in our own God-given way.

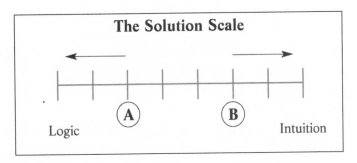

Although we're all different, each of us uses a combination of logic and intuition to analyze and solve difficulties:

- Those of us at the far end of the *intuitive or gut-instinct* scale use terms such as "I feel as though . . . " and "I believe . . . "
- Those of us on the *logical* side of the scale seek concrete facts, tending to analyze using a linear, systematic, step-by-step approach.
- The rest of us tend to be more *balanced and in the middle,* using both intuitive and logical analysis skills.

There's no right or wrong approach, but there is a best way. By using teams the more excellent method is to include both logical and intuitive approaches.

Problem solving is one of the best functions of task teams because such groups allow individuals at both ends of the scale to work together to view an obstacle from both the intuitive and the logical perspectives. Teaming tends to uncover the differences between symptoms, circumstances, and problems.

I'm naturally intuitive, so I approach situation dilemmas from that standpoint. That's not right or wrong; it's only my personal approach. A peer manager I worked with years ago used to chide me for my "feel good" approach to problem solving and decision-making. He was the analytical type and made decisions based on hard facts.

However, when either of us made decisions based solely on our *individual* temperaments, we made some good and some not-so-good decisions. When we made decisions together—relying on our abilities to come up with better solutions—we made many great decisions and solved severe crises.

His logical approach made my intuitive approach that much more valuable. However, it was slightly boring for me to listen to him take me step-by-step through his analysis. He couldn't understand how I could leap past logic and come to an answer. It wasn't easy for either of us, but we determined that we would learn to work together.

At one managers' meeting, I thought we would end up wrestling each other in the corner to decide who would win. Fortunately for us, other members of the team listened to both of us. In that meeting, we actually came out with a solution that incorporated the intuitive approach and the logical. Once we learned to appreciate each other, our difference in styles worked well for us for several years.

The Power of "Why?"

Regardless of our position on the solutions scale, we need one thing to excel at trouble analysis and resolution. It's a simple thing. We need to ask, "Why?"

Then we ask "Why?" again. And again. We keep on asking until it cannot be asked anymore.

Let's look at our Acme illustration again to see how it works:

Fact: People are not showing up at work on time or at all.
Question: Why?

Answer: Because we aren't giving them points and therefore they aren't being held accountable?

Analysis:

1. People don't stay home because they know we are not giving them points.

2. People stay at home because they don't like something on the job.

Conclusion: People staying home is a symptom of a larger dilemma.

Fact: Turnover is high.

Question: Why?

Answer: Because they don't like something about their job.

Question: Why?

Answer: Because their job is either not meaningful, doesn't provide competitive pay or benefits, or it doesn't allow for community or growth.

Analysis:

1. We are competitive in our pay and benefits.

2. We have good long-term career growth opportunities.

Conclusion: People are not finding meaning or community at Acme in Houston. Question: Why are people not finding meaning?

Answer: We are growing so fast that we may not be listening to what the employees are saying until it is too late. Our supervisors are not close enough to the employees to have clear and open lines of communication.

Question: Why?

Answer: Because their boss has created a culture that

devalues the employees, sacrifices productivity for caring, and
values performance more than people.

This illustration shows how we keep asking *why* until we
can't ask *why* anymore. We continue going back to the symptoms and allow the light to shine on the situation until we finally
grasp the core issue. Then we're ready to make changes. As
long as the difficulty lies masked by symptoms and circumstances, we are, essentially, applying what we call Band-aids to a
malady that needs surgery.

Applied Skills and Problem Solutions

Every skill we have presented is necessary if we are to become
Unconditionally Excellent at solving problems.

- Communications? A definite prerequisite.
- Teams? Absolutely a necessity.
- Follow-through? We can't fix anything if we don't
  finish.
- Initiative? Yes! Someone needs to take the initiative to
  solve difficult situations.
- Time/task reliability? Dependability and reliability
  alone could solve many difficulties.

Give me a single employee who is willing to develop her
maximum ability in these skill areas, and I'll be pleased. Have
her use these skills to become a problem solver, and I'll be

delighted. Give me more than one employee willing to do the same, and I'll be one of the most productive leaders in our organization. Give me a number of leaders with a similar number of employees committed to the same objective, and we will be unstoppable as a company.

Profitable? We will consistently outperform the competition.

Flexible? Bring on change. We'll show we're the best at adapting and adjusting to it.

A best place to work? The culture we create will keep the best employees and attract others of like mind and commitment. We will be a company that consistently produces results beyond being merely world class. I cannot underestimate the value we can bring to our bosses and supervisors and the impact we can have on our career when we put all of these skills together to become problem solvers.

So far we have focused on the F.I.T.—*F*ollow-through, *I*nitiative, and *T*ime-task. We have moved on to communication, teamwork, and problem-solving skills. All of these lead to Unconditional Excellence. But there are people with great skill sets that still lack the ingredients that make up Unconditional Excellence. In the next chapters, we'll focus on character skills that also impact Unconditional Excellence.

Where skills have degrees of competency, character is more of a Boolean value; either competence is, or it is not. The character traits that prove to be most valuable in becoming Unconditionally Excellent do not come in varying degrees, yet you do have the ability to develop your character skills.

chapter nine

Integrity

"I always hire character first and competency second." The speaker was Tom Hill, executive vice president of the Kimray Company in Oklahoma City. "Experience is a distant third." Tom is so committed to "character first" that he has spent much of his time, talent, and financial resources developing an institute that teaches character principles in schools, businesses, and government.

Competence, which is what we have dealt with thus far, is important. Competence is what people see first, but our ability to perform with excellence is based on character. Regardless of how competent we may be, trust will always be based on our character first. It is impossible, not merely difficult, to be Unconditionally Excellent without character.

Integrity, Not Balance

At the core of our character is integrity. Unfortunately for the business world of today we have lost the true meaning of the word. In a world of relativism, the word seems to have drifted to two different extremes. On the one hand, it means being open to and tolerant of others. On the other, it means living according to absolute truths, a set of absolute standards.

It can't be both. Or can it?

As I thought about *integrity*, it became obvious to me how misunderstood this word is. I also realized how rarely I hear the word used in the marketplace. I decided that's because this is the quality that most people call *honesty*.

The meaning certainly includes honesty, but the word *honesty* is inadequate. Here's my definition: *Integrity is living an integrated life, balanced between what we say we believe and what we actually do.*

"Oh, you mean *balance*?" someone said, noticing a single word when I made that statement. "You mean that if I just live a balanced life, then I'm all right?"

"That's not it," I said. "The problem is that we can't remain balanced. We find our equilibrium—but something always comes along to destabilize us."

The nature of most work environments today makes trying to live a balanced life a risky and impossible ideal. Living an integrated life, although it may be difficult to achieve, is far less likely to lead to discouragement, failure, and the sacrifice between our personal lives and our careers.

Perhaps a true story will help explain what I mean. Tony seemed to have life totally under his control and had gone upward in his career by doing what had to be done to succeed. He was the regional vice president of sales for a large insurance broker. His wife, Marilyn, supported him wholeheartedly, taking care of the kids, the house, and pretty much running the family while Tony built his career. He lived what I call the perfect "when I . . . then I" life.

- *"When I* finish this licensing course, *then I* can spend more time at home with the kids and you." He finished the course. He didn't spend more time at home.
- *"When I* close this one more account, *then I* will get the promotion that will let me take it easy for a while." He closed the account. He didn't rest.
- *"When I* get just one more agent hired, *then I* can turn over a lot of the selling functions to them and I can focus more on the kids and you." He hired the agent. He held on to his control.
- *"When I* hire a new office manager to replace Olivia, *then I* can slow down and focus on you and the kids." He hired Sharon. He didn't slow down.
- *"When I* make partner, *then I* can really slow down and spend more time doing the things we like to do and focus on some volunteer work, since the kids are off at college." He got the promotion. He didn't volunteer.

Most people easily get the point because it speaks closely to the lifestyles they themselves live. Like them, Tony always had something else he had to accomplish and *then* he would get his life back into harmony.

The most disruption in his life came when his wife said, "I want a divorce. You and I live in different worlds, and I can't play runner-up to your career any longer. The kids come second to you. I'm also angry because I let it happen. You left us behind you as you made your career plans, and I let you go on. I won't let that happen anymore."

The Inevitable Bump

Tony was one of the most honest men I know. When he shared his sad situation with me, I realized he had become one of the most disintegrated men I knew. His priority had become his career. When his career demanded more, he stabilized his life by giving up something—usually something to do with his family. When leadership demanded more, he balanced it by giving up time with his kids. When ownership demanded more, he juggled it by giving up time with his wife.

For Tony, the *Inevitable Bump*—the IB—was that heart-breaking conversation with his wife. Those devastating words from his wife forced Tony to know just how out of balance he had become. He later said that when she left him that's when he felt his life had gone completely out of control.

As I listened to his story, I thought of a spinning top I had when I was a kid. I watched in fascination as it began to rotate, smoothly twirling around and around, faster than the eye can follow. My toy kept doing that until it hit an IB, careened out of control, and fell over. No matter what I did, I couldn't ever make that top slow down gradually.

Neither could Tony.

Neither can the rest of us, because we can't shift directions of a spinning top.

For me, the IB came through a phone call during a sales presentation. I ran the southeastern regional sales and marketing division for Pennsylvania House. In the middle of that meeting, the phone rang and Brian Mock, my friend and coworker, hurriedly answered. Seldom does a hotel disturb a meeting by phone, knowing they might interrupt an important presentation.

Momentarily, Brian stepped out of the room.

When he walked back into the room and waved for my attention, irritation washed over me. I paused and stared at him, letting him know I wished he had ignored the call and allowed me to finish.

"Alan, they need you on the phone."

"Right! Tell them I'm too busy. I'll call back *after* the meeting."

"You need to take this call," he said firmly.

"I said—"

"It's about Sara."

The next minutes blur, but I stopped the presentation and picked up the phone.

"You don't know me," the voice said. "My name is Patricia, and I'm a nurse. I was just at the scene of an accident that your wife, your son, and your mother have had. First, let me tell you this. Sara is all right, although she is hurt badly. Your son is all right, and they are taking him to Scottish Rite Hospital. Your mother is also all right, but they are taking her to the emergency room at Northside Hospital."

"What about the baby?"

"You need to get to the hospital. The baby is under a lot of stress." She wouldn't say anything more than that.

At the time of the accident, Sara was eight months pregnant. Patrick, our three-year-old son, had been in the front seat, and my mother was in back. Sara, in deep trauma because of the accident, went into labor at the scene of the accident. The paramedics rushed her to Northside Hospital maternity unit. They took Patrick to Scottish Rite Children's Hospital, across the street. My mother was in the emergency room at Northside Hospital. All three of them had been hospitalized and each in a different place.

This balanced leader had no balance whatsoever.

As I drove to Northside Hospital to see Sara first, I thought of God's goodness that Sara really was all right. I prayed that our sons Patrick and Michael, who was yet to be born, would also be healthy.

At that moment, I would have sacrificed every business success and every financial gain for that not to be happening. What I thought was important was clearly out of balance with the priority that God had placed in my life.

My wife recovered after eight weeks in the hospital, our older son was fine, and so was my mother. Our second son was born by normal delivery.

I learned an invaluable lesson from that experience. Before that, I had made many plans for my life and especially for my career, and I was becoming increasingly successful. I was a bit stressed, but I assured myself that it was only a temporary imbalance. Then I hit my personal inevitable bump, or IB. Only later could I look back and think about that. We live in a world that constantly bumps us as we're spinning along, especially when we think we have our lives under control. When we hit the IB, we feel like a kid's top flying out of control that finally hits the wall and stops. The IB comes in moments of crisis. Sometimes it can be just the little, unexpected day-to-day things that throw us off schedule or frustrate us because we're on a tight time schedule.

We react in many different ways, and so does the world. So do the people upon whom we're trying to shine our lights. Because of who we are, we should have the answer for them when they hit the IB.

The sad part is, we don't. We get out of balance just like everybody else.

For others, the IB comes differently:

- "Our stock has gone down 23 percent this year. We're not only downsizing, we're eliminating your department."
- "I'm sorry, sir, but there has been a terrible accident," says the police officer on the other end of the line. "We need you to come down to the morgue and identify the body."
- "Business has been slow because of the sluggish economy. Instead of a bonus, we have to offer you a severance package of three months' pay."
- Or maybe it's when you get the results from a physical examination and the doctor says, "I have some very bad news . . . "

There's no way to escape the IBs. They will intrude and throw us off center. What we can do is to become such upright people that those things are only bumps and not crashes.

If we live purpose-filled lives and focus on balanced living and working for Unconditional Excellence, those bumps don't destroy us.

As I travel among business people, they often tell me their stories. I'm amazed at the common pattern I've discovered among the best of them.

"I thought I was doing the right thing. I made a lot of money and . . . " is a typical opening. I listen because I know that once the person has told me about all the achievements, I'll hear the word *but*, followed by the story of how that person hit his or her IB.

The best testimony, however, comes from those who were already upright, reliable individuals who spoke of Jesus Christ as the power that pulled them through. The IBs challenged them, but they didn't overwhelm them. Their circumstances changed and sometimes their careers faced setbacks, but their characters remained firm.

The Honesty Component

Two other components of integrity are character requirements of Unconditional Excellence. I call them *honesty with grace* and *honesty that hurts.*

Honesty with Grace

We live in a graceless, unforgiving world. Results count.

The corporate mentality doesn't accept problems or excuses.

How do we balance what we consider absolute truth in a relativistic society? Many religious people appear angry and judgmental. They are often quick to point out the error in the life of another. It can create huge tensions and problems at work.

Here's another true story. The president of a business had contracted with our company, Corporate Development Institute (CDI), for help developing a culture of Unconditional Excellence. Cindy was in charge of their information systems. She had her share of problems and issues, such as not being a player when the job required a team effort. She worked by her own rules when it came to things like overtime, implying to coworkers that those regulations referred to others but not to her. Cindy never taught others how to solve problems, because being a problem solver gave her a sense of power and made her indispensable to anyone who needed her help.

Although she was extremely capable, she was not interdependent. That fact didn't go unnoticed by several members of our leadership team. "Cindy is like the missing cog in the flow of meaningful information," one of them said. "She causes problems in every area of the organization," said another.

That second statement prompted us to move into action. Once we admitted that this was more than a problem within a contained area, we knew we had to act.

When we discussed how to handle the problem, I sensed another issue lying close to the surface that had not yet come out. It was one of those gut reactions to what was going on. I waited and probed. Finally, the accounting manager said,

"There's something else."

As he began to speak, Cindy's supervisor nodded. He, too, had known.

"Cindy has abused her position and become very demanding because she has been involved with the vice president of marketing. She acts as if she is untouchable and she really is."

"She's like the elephant in the room that none of us can acknowledge," the second person said.

Everyone in that room knew that the vice president of marketing was a church leader and a man who took great pride in his spiritual commitment. I remembered coming on board as a consultant and reading their Mission Statement for Operation. He pointed out his major contribution, the item that read: "We will be people of integrity."

I needed to talk to the president before we could resolve the issue. I went into his office and told him what I learned and that all the executives were aware of the situation. They assumed others in the organization knew.

"What should we do?" he asked.

"Call a meeting with the other three vice presidents, and I'll be there as well."

He set up the meeting for the next day. Before the meeting, I met privately with the marketing vice president.

"You don't know what you're talking about!" he said. "How dare you listen to such gossip!"

"Everyone on the executive team knows. Maybe others do, too."

His belligerence and defensiveness made it difficult, but he finally admitted to the affair. Then he tried to justify it. "It happened only because my own marriage has been on the rocks for so long." He told me the sad story of his dysfunctional marriage.

"I'm sorry your life is miserable," I said—and meant it. "But this is business. You are supposed to be a man of moral principles and to set an example."

He turned his head away from me and said nothing.

The next morning when we met, I told the others that he had admitted to the allegations. "How do we handle this situation?" I asked.

The team began to make tentative suggestions. This was new territory for them. The harshest response came from the head of accounting. He was the most openly religious leader. "It's very clear to me. We need to fire them both. And we need to do it today!"

"That's drastic," the plant manager said. "I recommend that he go. He was the one in authority and I don't think his behavior is excusable. I think we should put Cindy on probation."

The fact that the affair had an impact on the performance and productivity of many people made the problem more complex than just the affair itself. As communication became more strained, trust, motivation, and performance deteriorated. The question was one of solving the problem, not the *symptom* of the problem. If the affair ended, would trust be restored and in turn would productivity increase?

"What do you think, Amy?" She was Cindy's direct supervisor, the office manager. She had taken the most abuse and had the most to gain from Cindy's dismissal. She stared into space for a few minutes and then said slowly, "I would like to work with Cindy to see if she can be salvaged. Despite all her problems, she's bright and a good worker. We may be able to turn it around if she'll let me help her."

That seemed satisfactory to us.

Amy turned to the president and said, "I think you owe him [the marketing vice president] the same opportunity. Give him a chance to fix it."

Before anyone could object, she added, "You allowed him the freedom to get into this mess. All of us knew what was going on—or at least suspected it—and we let it slip by. We knew but we didn't act honestly or out of principle, so we have some fault here as well. We lacked the courage and conviction to deal with the problem, because we were all more afraid of our own positions. We have to take some of the responsibility."

Amy had said everything that needed saying and she said it well. I couldn't find a better example of *honesty with grace* than that response. The religionist in us would demand justice; the graciousness in us demands justice with mercy.

The marketing vice president got a chance, but he found it impossible to work together with Cindy. Once the affair was open knowledge, she became his enemy and he treated her abusively. Within a month he was terminated.

Cindy received an opportunity to redeem herself and she promised she would. But despite repeated attempts to help her learn how to be a team player and support the rest of the company, she seemed unable to adjust. After the vice president's termination she turned defensive, resentful, and destructive. She was dismissed, also.

I wish the situation had ended better. Regardless of the outcome, however, the process was valuable, because all of the leaders learned something. Amy, the office manager, has become an even stronger leader. The team works better together than ever before. Because of that, they were able to take a stronger stand for uprightness and living by ethical principles. Our initial reaction to a situation that threatens us is often a rigid attitude based on what we know as right and wrong. In contrast, the better response usually comes from looking not only at what is right but also at how we might best do the right thing.

This brings us to a significant question: *What happens when people fail?* I mean failure at all levels, not just those involving moral or ethical issues.

I ask because I've watched the way people react to failure. We mark those who fail as lazy, incompetent, liars, cheats, thieves, or philanderers when in fact they are merely people who did not meet their obligations. Maybe they were inefficient at a task, or maybe they lied, cheated, stole, or fooled around. I hope the difference is obvious. When we brand people, we often mark them for life—at least for their life in that organization. Quite likely, they take that stigma with them to their next job or their promotion within the company.

There are situations that call for immediate and harsh action, such as when a lack of integrity puts others in dangerous situations or threatens the profitability of the business. Even in those situations, the way we address the issue is critical. Too often we apply justice when we need to offer mercy. Isn't it just possible that our organization could be served best and that our examples as people of honor and principle would be more compelling if we applied *both* justice and mercy?

I couldn't say for sure where Amy, from the illustration above, is in her faith. Although it was a Christian company, we never discussed that aspect of her life. Others in the same company, however, act as if they are not true followers unless they quote Bible verses or talk to someone every day about Jesus Christ. I do know this much about Amy: Her example of Unconditional Excellence not only impacted Cindy and her own life, but it influenced the rest of the company. She understood justice and that both of the parties *deserved* immediate termination, but she also advocated mercy—giving them what they did not deserve. That is a person in the workplace with the highest sense of ethics.

Honesty That Hurts

The second component of integrity is what I call "honesty that hurts." At times in our careers we're asked to act in ways that aren't consistent with our ethical standards. The situation begins when we're asked to make a small compromise. As we know, especially with hindsight, small concessions lead to larger ones and can result in outright fraud if left unchecked.

For most of us, however, compromise belongs in the little-white-lie category. What begins as something quite small can become a way of life. Our willingness to compromise continues growing until we develop a character flaw—a personal character defect, yes, but also a flaw in the personality of the company itself.

We can see compromise going on at any level. One of the easiest places to point it out is in the area of sales and marketing. The line between promotion, embellishment, and outright lying should be as wide as a three-lane highway. Unfortunately, we have a tendency to put all three in a narrow, two-lane road, where it's easy to get confused and cross the yellow line.

Trouble looms when people of integrity compromise on the little things. I want to make sure I'm clear about the word *compromise*. There are times we give in to cooperate, even if it's not the way we would do things. We do such acquiescing for the good of the company, for ourselves, and as part of the team. This kind of acquiescence doesn't involve giving up our principles or denying our value. Instead, we cooperate and bring about mutually satisfactory solutions. Compromise in situations such as these indicates that we are people of high principle because we can lay aside or surrender those things that don't threaten our values. Such an attitude also shows we want the best for the company, even if we don't agree.

In its bad sense, compromise refers to anything that devalues us as individuals, undermines the company, or harms another person. I want to share an example of honesty that hurts that is also a story of excellence.

In working with the S. D. Myers Company, one of the guiding principles we focused on was to honor God by being people of the highest caliber. A team from S. D. Myers joined teams from several of another company's plants, including the key managers. Previously, that company had been one of Myers' biggest competitors, but they had gone into Chapter 11. The reason for visiting was the possibility that Myers might acquire its competitor's assets. Of course, there were nondisclosure forms and legal documents to keep information from being used against the competitor. The leadership team was hesitant to share information with Myers that might come back to haunt them.

The Myers people needed valid information to make a realistic bid. Millions of dollars and hundreds of jobs were at stake. For the most part, Myers was able to work with the business broker to get our questions answered and to receive enough information needed to make a good offer.

At the executive leadership meeting Myers held to review the information and make a decision, one of the key concerns was who the other bidders might be. Sometimes, by not bidding, businesses allow other competitors to buy low so they can come into their territory and become the buyer's big competitor. Obviously, it helps to put a bid together if you know who the other potential bidders are.

Throughout the day at the facilities of the Chapter 11 company, every leader we met with was careful not to divulge any information concerning other potential bidders.

At the end of our visit, Dale Bissonette, the Myers CFO, asked bluntly, "Can you tell us who else is visiting this week or who else has expressed an interest?"

"I'm sorry, but I can't share that information," the broker said. That was the right thing to say.

We sat around the table guessing who it might be, when one of the team members turned to Ed Matheeny, the national sales manager, and said, "You used to work for Ron over at the Cleveland plant, right? What would you think about giving him a call and asking him who else came for the tour?" Before anyone answered, the team member said, "It sounds like all of us were impressed with Ron. If he tells Ed, he would be doing himself and us a favor. If we win the bid, he'll be working for us."

While Ed pondered the question, he took several deep breaths, and I could see that he was carefully weighing his response. Since I was involved as an outside consultant to assist Myers in developing the culture of Unconditional Excellence, I was interested in hearing how Ed would answer.

He shook his head slowly. "I can't do that. In the first place, I wouldn't ask him. In the second place, he wouldn't tell me. In the third place, if he did, we wouldn't want him working here, would we?"

"Good answer," Dana Myers, the CEO, said. "If we have to ask a man to violate his honor to save us a few dollars, we might as well change our vision."

I don't need to point out how many business people wouldn't have hesitated to make the phone call.

They could easily justify their actions by saying:

- "If we don't, it's going to cost us more money."
- "We might not be able to take over the company."
- "All of us win by our doing this. We become bigger and more profitable."

- "Everybody does it. Hey, I'm sure the others will do whatever they can to find out that we've been there."
- "It's no big deal, really."

The last response is crucial. It *is* a big deal. It is exactly at "minor" points such as this that compromise with principles begins.

Ed Matheeny stood for integrity, and Dana Myers backed him up. When I told this story to one business owner, he sneered, "Stupid way to do business. Those are the things that will hurt a company and stop their growth. Who cares where or how you get the information?"

He didn't get it.

The Cost of Integrity

Even if it hurts us at the moment, hinders our growth, or slows down our profitability, we have made a mark of Unconditional Excellence when we do the right thing. When we make a decision with integrity, regardless of the cost, it is right.

I want to emphasize one reason we struggle with compromise. It usually involves small things. They are things we can get away with and nobody, we assume, will know care. Integrity may cost us, and I think that's important to point out. Here are common areas where integrity can cost us:

- When we promise a customer a realistic delivery date. We know that our competitor will promise an earlier date—one they can't meet and they commit to something they cannot do. We lose the order.

- When we quote a customer the true cost of a proposal. Even as we give the figures, we know a competitor that will quote a lower price, then use "add-ons" to make the margin. If we were competing head-to-head we would win, but we don't use add-on pricing tactics. We lose the order.

- When we provide true specifications for what our product or service will do. We refuse to embellish to the point of potential dishonesty because we know our competitor's product can't do it either—but they claim it can. We lose the order.

- When we share the real story with a prospective new employee. We let her know the upside and the downside of the new job so she has no serious surprises. A competing company promises her working conditions and perks they know they can't provide. We lose a potentially good employee.

- When we tell a customer, "We cannot hit this deadline." That customer threatens to cancel because as a buyer all he needs is a "delivery promise" to keep his boss off his back. "I know you can't hit that date, but I can deal with that later." We refuse to give him a date. We lose a large order from that customer.

The list is endless and it might seem daunting. Yet the net effect of making decisions with integrity is that we establish a culture that our customers, employees, and suppliers can value. Employees flourish and thrive in such a culture.

We live in a universe of eventual justice. God honors us when we choose integrity. When we stand for the right things, *people know*. Our reputation spreads. We may lose one deal, but we might gain our souls in the process. Over a period of time, even the losses we encounter seem to turn around and become gains. The order we lost to someone becomes a larger and better order in the future because the customer knows we are reliable, honorable people.

The buyer who loses confidence in us and cancels the order regains that confidence when he has to make a decision based on integrity rather than expedience. The potential employee we lost may one day be the employee we gain because she has decided to make a career move and join a company with a history of integrity.

The long-term effect of our decisions may be good—and it may not be! That's part of the risk involved in making such decisions. We still need to do the right thing even if it means we lose in the short run. Sometimes we never see an upside when we make the honorable decision. We do the right thing because it is the right thing, and we may suffer a loss as a result. Someone else gets the promotion because she hit their numbers, even if she lied to customers to do it.

We have no guarantee that doing the right thing will always turn out well, but the foundation we lay when we act with integrity is one of the most important aspects of the character of Unconditional Excellence. It is the rock on which we build the foundation of our lives. When tested, only those lives built on solid foundations will stand.

Let's not miss what is possibly the best reason for building our competency in Unconditional Excellence on an ethical platform. The world not only watches *what* we do but *how* we do it. People talk, word spreads, and reputations change. In any business or industry, most people know the companies they can trust.

As people who confess faith in Christ, we are called to live according to a standard that is clearly above normal, acceptable standards. What we say we believe will be made more evident by how we behave than by what we speak.

I can know and speak all the right words and still pollute the truth. If I tell people I base my life on honoring God by living a life of integrity, I dishonor God when I act in a way that lacks uprightness.

It saddens me when I attend conferences or make speeches and hear from business leaders, many of whom are professing Christians, that some of the worst employees they have are believers. They sometimes say they avoid doing business with other Christians who constantly talk about their faith, display their commitment in terms of a fish symbol on their cars, or send evangelistic e-mail messages to coworkers who don't want to read them.

I don't understand those who live with an outward façade of religion and yet show so little commitment in their attitude and work. I do understand those whose lives proclaim their values and faith, even if they don't articulate them well.

The apostle Paul was a tent maker. I doubt that his tents

leaked and I'll bet he never made a customer commitment that he did not keep. Jesus was a carpenter; I'll bet his benches held up and that he, too, never made delivery promises that he did not keep. I can't believe that Peter the fisherman slipped day-old fish among the fresh catch of the day.

As employees or leaders, are we called to anything less than the same standard?

chapter ten

The Strength of Humility in Leadership

66**T**here isn't a lot of room for humility in this company." The speaker was Reg, my boss, the vice president of sales and marketing. I've mentioned Reg earlier.

The Humility Factor

Under Reg, the sales at our company had grown at an impressive 35 percent annual rate for three consecutive years. The figure becomes even more significant when I point out that it happened at a time the industry itself was growing at a rate of only 6 percent. Our profitability was consistently between 18 and 20 percent EBIT (Earnings Before Interest and Taxes) in an industry that averaged 9 percent.

"The salespeople sitting in this room have made the biggest contribution to the success of this company," Reg said, smiling. "And I hired almost every one of you. You are cocky, you are confident, and you are good at what you do."

The listeners included not only the sales and marketing department but also the CEO and department heads from the rest of the company.

"We make a lot of money for our shareholders, and we make a lot of money for ourselves. We ought to! We're good."

So far, that was vintage, arrogant Reg.

"I've been asked by the folks in manufacturing if we would focus more on the underperforming plants and lay off giving orders to our Lewisburg plant because we're burying them." He paused and laughed. "We are oversold out of that plant. They can forget it if they can't keep up." Reg paused and stared directly at the CEO. "Fire them and get some leaders who can make things happen at Lewisburg!"

He turned his attention to us once again and said, "Bury them! Sell everything and anything you can. This is not a time to slow down and make excuses. You may be the best there are, but remember, I brought you into this company, and I can take you out of it." With that he closed the sales meeting and opened the bar.

For several minutes he had been railing against those in the company who didn't live up to his expectations or perform as he believed they should. I sat in shocked silence. I couldn't believe what I had just heard.

A regional sales manager sitting next to me just laughed. "That's old Reg. He hasn't changed," he said and shook his head. "And I wouldn't have expected anything else."

This was the first time I had been to the annual meeting. I glanced at the vice president of manufacturing. He had obviously felt the sting of Reg's harshness and his face still showed it. The CEO, however, seemed to have enjoyed Reg's remarks.

I was embarrassed and so were others. In his remarks Reg had singled me out by name as one of the sales people he had recruited. Now he was challenging me to bury my peers in manufacturing.

This really happened, except that I've left out the direct expletives Reg used to describe the folks in manufacturing.

As shocking as this may sound to some—especially given that Reg could have been far more honest and arrogant in his directions to us—Reg's type is not that uncommon in business. Most of the time, however, they're not as blatant.

I didn't know it when Reg spoke, but behind the scenes a power struggle was raging. The current CEO was moving up to the parent company, and either Reg or Gary, the vice president of manufacturing, would be promoted. As I said in an earlier chapter, Reg got the job.

Under Reg's leadership, most of the real champions in the company left within three years, and the company lost more than half its business. Knowledgeable people in the industry and most customers attributed the company's failure to Reg's arrogance and lack of concern for anyone other than himself.

I call it a lack of humility.

Is there room for humility in the business world today, or is it as Reg said? Let's look at the example of Peter Drucker. Many people, including me, consider him to be the father of modern-day leadership principles. He doesn't use the word "humility," but he makes a good case for its importance in business, especially in the area of leadership.

Drucker focuses on one aspect of leadership. I would like

to address the broader concept of leadership authority, which is available to every employee in an organization, regardless of his or her job title or position. While this book is not a leadership book, there is a responsibility for each of us to play a leadership role, regardless of our position in the company.

What do I mean by humility? I define the word to mean *using our strengths to bring out the best in others for the good of the whole.*

Think about that for a moment. Doesn't it fly in the face of what we traditionally think of as humility? I have asked many groups to define the word for me. Far too often I hear words like weak, mild-mannered, timid, or meek. Many assume humility means allowing people to get away with anything or shutting up and making no protest over wrongdoing. In reality, humility means recognizing that everything we are and everything we have comes from God.

Humility is a powerful quality that's based on our strengths and not our weaknesses. It focuses us and allows us to bring out the best in others, not for selfish gain but for the best of everyone.

I see little humility in our self-promotional, self-indulgent business environment. When I do spot humility, I see it in those whose lives and lifestyles have positively influenced the business itself and the careers of other employees.

A Living Example

Trent Bieghle is a powerful example, an entry-level employee who, through his Unconditional Excellence, became the president of his company. Trent is a talented man, but I believe it was his humility that stood out more than anything else.

While he was still in high school, he started working for Black & White Technologies. The owners, Ken and Judy White, recognized his potential. Trent drove a pickup truck part-time, delivered material to job sites, and picked up supplies when needed. He was a glorified gofer.

Trent enrolled full-time in an engineering school and continued to work for them. He went from being a gofer to scheduling and handling odd jobs in the office. His skills grew as he learned engineering. He became continually more valuable as an employee.

After Trent was graduated from college, he became the head of Black & White's engineering department. All the way he backed the owners, the crew chief, and anyone else he came into contact with on the job. Everyone liked and trusted Trent. He's a deeply committed Christian who surrendered his strengths and used them to benefit other people. Trent also made it clear that eventually he wanted to own his own business and that he would leave the company.

A few years later, Ken and Judy White faced the serious decision of whether to retire. Should they turn the company over to their son? The son didn't want to run the company. While it's usually a foregone conclusion in most similar situations that the son would be elevated to the position of president, Ken and Judy wanted to do what was in the best interest of all of the employees of Black & White, and not just for themselves or their son. They decided to offer the company and the presidency to Trent, who would pay them for their company out of future profits.

I am honored to have served on their board for several years, and I can tell you that I have never seen a better example of bringing out the best in others than I have seen during my work with Black & White Technologies.

I would be hard-pressed to decide who exhibits humility better—Ken and Judy White or Trent Bieghle. One thing is certain. They have established a leadership with the foundation of Unconditional Excellence that many company owners only dream about.

Some might say, "Oh, sure, once you're in a position of power, you can do all kinds of things."

Trent was the part-time gofer, the lowest in the company where he began to establish himself. The commitment to give his best and to bring out the best in others wasn't an idea Trent acquired after he climbed the ladder. He established himself when he had no personal power.

If Trent could do it, doesn't it make sense to say that anyone *at any level* could do it? All of us may not have the same opportunities or end up in key positions, but we can still see the benefits throughout our career.

Humility, like the characteristic of sponsoring champions (which I speak about in the next chapter), is a synergistic attribute. That means that the more people manifest such a quality, the more impact it has on others.

Here's another way of saying it. The results of humility are not additive in an organization but geometric. An explosion of excellence occurs that can have far-reaching effect on the performance and profitability of the company. This can happen because we use our combined strengths for the benefit of all. Individual strengths combine with others to develop and multiply others' talents. That results in a multiplied effect. Two plus ten comes to just twelve, but two raised to the tenth power is one thousand twenty-four. The idea of seeking the best in others for the good of all can be that powerful.

Unfortunately for most companies, too few employees commit themselves to using their abilities to bring out the best in others. Similarly, too many employees use their talents for their good alone. Isn't it typical of organizations that a few stand out because they perform at a level far above the norm? The rest of the employees plod along, doing what is expected.

We can release within a company a collective effort that leads to a standard of exceptional performance. Individual employees probably can't do it alone, but one employee can start the process.

Not only do I believe in humility, but I also believe it's a crucial quality for any one who aspires to be the best. It is just as crucial in any organization that strives for Unconditional Excellence.

Bringing out the best in others for the good of all is based on our ability to lead, which comes to us through the appointment to a position of leadership. Even though many of us aren't in positions of leadership, one of the most important roles we have as employees is in our commitment to Unconditional Excellence.

Self-Promotion

"If I don't promote myself, who will?" That's what I hear. "If I don't toot my own horn, how will I get noticed? If I don't look out for number one, will I become number two or number ten?"

More than once I've been laughed at and had to listen to people quote the most famous Bible verse that's not in the Bible: "God helps those who help themselves." The truth is, God helps those who help others.

It's really doing the right thing for the right reasons for the most good. I especially want to emphasize the last phrase: for the most good.

I put this strongly because I feel strongly. For me, humility means that I am willing to let God become my promoter. This quality isn't passive. It doesn't presuppose the absence of activity. It means that I work hard and do everything I can for those who employ me, but it doesn't mean that I give my best just to be commended, rewarded, or promoted. I keep in mind the good of the entire organization.

When I struggle to self-promote, I usually end up harming others, using others, or ignoring others. Self-promoting nearly always involves attempting to demote others so I harm them and myself.

By serving others, through our strengths and divinely given gifts, God will receive the credit in a world that screams, "I did it, and therefore I should be rewarded." If we never get the recognition in terms of promotion or pay increases, we can still be absolutely certain that God will reward us in his way and in his time.

If we allow God to work in us so that at every opportunity we shine bright lights in every corner of darkness, we lose interest in pointing the light at ourselves or calling attention to ourselves. With that attitude, we can change the entire nature of the relationship with those we have contact with.

I can hear someone protest by saying, "But if we just sit back and don't promote ourselves and our product, we'll go out of business." Of course we have to work hard, and we need to promote our products. I advocate honest marketing and salesmanship. What I'm raising my voice against is *self*-promotion. We need to learn to give up being recognized or applauded for our efforts.

"How will I ever get a raise? If I don't get a raise, I won't be able to show the goodness of God." That's such a limited concept. We show God's goodness by our attitude, our Unconditional Excellence, the quality of our work, and our lives. We all want raises in pay, but promoting ourselves and blowing trumpets every time we do something outstanding isn't the way of Unconditional Excellence.

Self-Denial

Humility means we make use of the strengths and the gifts that God has given us. This doesn't mean we put ourselves down or deny what we can do.

For example, I'm a good speaker. I have the ability—a gift—to energize people, get them excited, and open them to possibilities around them. That's not bragging. It's a statement that admits my ability came to me from God. Whatever talents I have, I didn't give to myself. I could have said, "Well, you know, I'm not really very good at this, I just try hard." That may sound self-deprecating and like I'm not a pride-filled person, but it's pseudo-humility.

We need to learn to acknowledge what we can do—and admit God gives us that ability. If we play the game of "I can't do much," or "I'm not very good at this," we dishonor God.

Four Types of Authority

When we practice humility in the workplace, we also become people of authority. I want to point out four ways we receive leadership authority:

1. Positional Authority

This comes with a title and a leadership job description. We might be a frontline supervisor or the CEO. The responsibility to lead was granted with the position. The job title makes it clear who we are to lead and what we are to accomplish.

If my title is vice president of sales, it would be safe to assume I am responsible for leading the sales force. If I am the production manager, it's a good bet I am over the workers on the production line or the supervisors that they report to.

2. Halo Authority

This means we are near someone with positional authority. Janice is the best example I know. While her official title is executive secretary, it is her unique relationship to Smith Lanier, the chairman and CEO of J. Smith Lanier and Company, which gives her that halo authority.

If halo authority is abused it becomes "politics" and a negative power used for personal gain rather than as a force for good. I have conducted seminars for the employees in Janice's office and after I defined halo authority I asked them to think of someone who used their authority well. Janice was the immediate and nearly unanimous response.

3. Competency Authority

This is derived from neither our immediate job nor our position near someone with positional authority. It grows out of competence. Many assume that competence is a trait all positional leaders possess. My assumption, however, is that most of us have worked for an incompetent leader. We may even have thought or said, "I wonder how in the world he got the position in the first place."

For every employee who has an opportunity to lead without halo or positional authority, competence can earn them their authority. Other employees follow coworkers if they know that employee is knowledgeable and competent. As we work on the applied skills of Unconditional Excellence, we increase our competency authority.

4. Character Authority

This is closely aligned with competency authority, but it emanates from the strength of our character. Again, we would like to assume that everyone in leadership positions has character authority; quite often, though, that's not the case in the business world. Hal was a perfect example of a positional leader with great competence authority and little character authority. That defect turned out to be his downfall. Unfortunately for the hundreds of people who lost their jobs as a direct result of his poor leadership, the company reacted too late for them.

Does Humility Work?

I have one illustration that happened at a company I worked with as I was developing the "Unconditional Excellence" seminar. I asked employees participating in the seminar to share experiences that illustrated any of the principles we talked about. Most of the time, people shared excellent examples that related to their current peer group. Most negative examples dealt with past experiences or people in other areas of the company.

In one session Belinda shared what started out to be a great example of working for the good of others. Here is her story.

"When I first started here, I had a hard time closing out some of the accounts in the computer. I wasn't familiar with the system and I had a hard time following the IT department's processes. I was frustrated and unhappy and found myself working late just trying to stay caught up. I really thought I was in over my head, to the point that I was about to go tell Rick I couldn't do the job."

Belinda continued. "One early evening, when I was at my wit's end, one of the other account managers came into my cubicle and asked if there was anything she could do. Since most of the rest of the employees had already gone home, I was reluctant to share my burden because I knew she wanted to go home, too. I guess my frustration level was too high, because I actually broke down in tears."

I knew it was hard on her, sharing these deep emotions with her peers looking on. But she persevered. "Once the other account manager realized what I was having trouble with, she showed me a few shortcuts that she had developed over the years that made the job so much simpler and faster. I wondered why the IT people didn't know these tricks and if anyone else had the same problems I had."

As I listened, I slowly began to understand that maybe this wasn't going to be a positive example, but I let her continue. Since all of the other account managers were in the room, I also knew that the woman who had helped Belinda had either left the company or was sitting in the room listening to this story. The latter proved to be the case.

"I really did appreciate the help. I ended up being able to leave within fifteen minutes of most of the other account managers and I realized there must be more tricks of the trade I could learn to help me be more effective. I was going to go in to our managing director, Rick, and tell him about the help the other account manager gave me and see if maybe we could all sit down and find out how we could do a better job by sharing our trade secrets.

"When I asked him if we could meet, he told me he had wanted to talk with me, also, and discuss my progress. As soon as I sat down, he told me he was sorry to hear that I was having trouble with the computer and that if I needed any additional help I could ask the account manager who helped me with the closing out issues."

The account manager who had appeared to be helping had actually gone behind Belinda's back with reports of her weakness.

She paused and lowered her head. She seemed to be very angry or very hurt. Maybe both.

"When you shared with us that humility was about sharing your strengths to bring out the best in others, I thought about how close this was to being a good example. Maybe that's right and maybe it works in some places. It doesn't work here. In reality, what I've seen is selfishness and looking out for number one." She brushed the tears from her eyes. "You know, I never did go back and ask that person for help again. Here in this office we pretty much look out for our own interests. It's too risky to trust someone else to look out for our best interest."

Most of the account managers were staring at the table in front of them. Any of them in that room could have been the offending culprit. Instead of bringing out the best in Belinda, that other person feathered her own cap in her boss' eyes, and she did it at Belinda's expense.

I broke the silence. "I wonder how much impact you could have on your performance and your productivity if you all shared your knowledge, not only with each other but with IT so they could train the other ten offices?"

Later I learned that Jenny, the account manager who had "helped" Belinda, came to her and asked for forgiveness. She did it in front of Rick, and that made it even more meaningful. Out of this process came an account manager task team whose focus was improving productivity by developing a systemwide training program. The task team was made up of account managers from every office, as well as representatives from the IT department. Belinda and Jenny both served on it. They are rebuilding the bonds of trust and learning how to use their individual strengths to bring out the best in others for the good of the entire organization.

As I write these words, I can report that their company has been recognized by the industry's most significant publications and by their suppliers as one of the fastest growing and most profitable in their industry. Their industry magazine has hailed them as a "company of excellence."

Humility is like that. It is a spark that creates a flame that turns into a fire. I'm learning—still learning—that if I use my talent without being concerned for God, people will like what I say, and I'll have many fans. I'll self-promote. I'll want to hear them say, "You're so wise. You have just the answers I need." However, I would much rather have people come up to me and say, "God spoke to me through you. That really affected me."

This doesn't mean that everything will go the way we want. As we allow God to promote us, we get to that core of humility. To get there, we have to trust that this is what God wants and that God is the ultimate promoter.

It's very difficult in a materialistic, commercial, and self-promoting society to think and talk that way. In the marketplace, the entire capitalist system is juxtaposed from that platform by 180 degrees. I suspect that if I tried to present the concept of humility to the Harvard Business School, most of the professionals there would laugh at me. God's way has never been the most popular.

I'd like to raise up an army of people who seek to let God direct their careers and their business opportunities for the good of the entire organization. I am finding a few such people. Some are CEOs; others are vice presidents. I've met outstanding supervisors and file clerks. They all have one thing in common: They believe that God has put them in their current positions. They didn't self-promote or step on anyone to get there. They are the true bright lights.

Our Examples

Once I caught on to the principle of humility, I began to think about people in the Bible. It amazed me to see that none of the great biblical leaders ever promoted themselves. David never sought to be king, even when he could easily have killed King Saul. Joseph, even in an Egyptian prison, never did anything to promote himself. God had to give Moses several assurances before he rose to leadership. Joshua faithfully served Moses even before the divine tap came for him to succeed the great leader. Daniel took his stand against the evils of Babylon and God still promoted him as well as the three young men who refused to bow to an idol.

When I read about those powerful leaders, it gives me hope. It lets me know that I don't have to run the company—I only have to remember to use my strengths to bring out the best in others for the good of the whole.

chapter eleven

Sponsoring Champions

Shortly after I became owner of my own company, Design South Furniture, I noticed a young man named Darren Dickerson. He had become the supervisor in shipping. Darren was one of those people who makes it a joy to be around him.

As I watched him over a period of weeks, I realized that although he did an excellent job in shipping, he showed more potential than the job demanded. I began to mentor and prepare him to move up at Design South.

He exceeded my initial hopes. Within six months, he had become the plant manager and, as usual, his work was excellent. Several years later, Darren received an offer to work for a larger company where he would receive a large increase in pay and a benefits package that a small company like ours couldn't match. He had a growing family, so I advised him that as much as we hated to lose him, I didn't think we could offer him the kind of growth opportunities the other company could. He decided to take the job.

The day before he left our company, Darren came to my office. "Most of what I learned in order to take this promotion, you taught me."

It was a bittersweet experience for me. He was right, but Darren would have learned it from someone else if I hadn't been around. Champions will always grow—it just takes time and the right environment. We help those talented individuals by sponsoring them.

Jesus provides us with a powerful example of the sponsorship of champions. The twelve disciples were his choices. As far as we know, none of them had done anything outstanding previously, but Jesus recognized the potential in them—probably possibilities that even they could not see.

He spent three years preparing a group of second-class citizens, ticked off the religious establishment, and upset the Roman leaders. In his final instructions to his small band, what he said, in effect, was, "I've taught you, and I've lived the example I want you to follow. Now you handle it." I love the kind of confidence he had in them—the same kind of confidence he shows in us today.

Sponsoring the best creates an interesting tension: What happens if we promote people beyond their ability in our department, division, or even within our business? Darren's story illustrates what can happen when we back a winner.

When we mentor those talented individuals, we can't always retain them in our company. Would we still support them if we knew that by doing so we would lose those winners?

Yes! If we're truly those who encourage and support others, we do it because it is the right thing to do.

When I tell the story of Darren, I nearly always get this

response: "But he quit your company!"

Often they add, "You might have been better served by sponsoring someone who wouldn't leave you."

I don't agree. Darren left a legacy of excellence. He also raised up winners who are still in place and making outstanding contributions. It is no mistake to sponsor someone we may lose down the road.

There's one secret about backing champions, and Darren exemplifies it. We don't get behind a potential winner just to make our company better or more profitable. We do it for *them*. We seek their good—and their good may mean they will go elsewhere. When we encourage and help with that spirit, those we get behind make our businesses more productive and profitable, and their impact lasts even after they are gone.

Darren moved on because our organization wasn't big enough to contain a man of his ability. Despite my personal sense of loss, I can honestly say that it delighted me that he shared his excellence at his new company.

Sponsoring Clark Kent and Finding Superman

Those whom I call true champions are different from the average worker. Not only are they steady performers, they're also the ones with that extra spark—that something that makes them stand out. Quite obviously, the qualities that make them stand out are the attributes I've already pointed out in this book.

True champions are Unconditionally Excellent employees.

They do the things I've written about, and they commit themselves to growing and making long-term contributions to the world of business.

These stars excel at what they do. They keep learning, and they make the most of their opportunities. This year they may perform at a high level; next year, they're likely to raise their own standards. They're committed to meeting or exceeding that ever-increasing standard. The status quo and last year's accomplishments are never good enough.

Why don't we see and hear more about these outstanding individuals? Maybe an illustration will help. As a kid, I loved watching Superman on television, but one thing about the show always troubled me. Why was everyone in Metropolis so stupid that none of them recognized that Clark Kent was really Superman? To become Clark Kent, all Superman had to do was put on a suit, a pair of glasses, and act like a nerd. What kind of disguise was that?

The truth is, our business-world supermen aren't that well disguised either. Most of the time they don't try to hide their superpowers. (Why should they?) Our responsibility is to help them find their own phone booth to make the change so that we can work together to create an environment conducive to success. Then we pull back and gaze in awe as they cry out, "Up, up, and away!"

The champion is a strong biblical concept. Jesus not only did it, but the disciples sought out their champions. One of the interesting and little-noticed stories is that in the early church a strong leader named Barnabas sponsored Paul, who had once persecuted the faith. On at least two occasions, Barnabas had to step in for him. Paul in his turn got behind Timothy and urged him to mentor others.

My favorite story is that of a young follower named John Mark who left Paul and Barnabas on their first trip to take the Gospel outside of the Holy Land. Later, the young man wanted another chance, and Paul said no. Barnabas said yes—even if it meant arguing with Paul. John Mark is one of the four acknowledged gospel writers, author of the book of Mark. Paul later called John Mark "profitable." Barnabas' instincts paid off.

Even as we say, "Hooray for Superman," we should remember that for every superman or superwoman, we probably employ ten "Steady Eddies." Those are our faithful, plodding performers who won't ever be star quality, but who will perform to a high level consistently. Companies thrive on those steady workers.

We don't sponsor them to the same level we sponsor champions, but we must give them every opportunity for career growth and meaningful work. As leaders decide how to use their time, talents, and resources, they must be careful to allocate their time to sponsor every employee.

Two Types of Champion

In Chapter 7, I made a distinction between original and synthetic creativity. A similar distinction also holds true here. I call the types *Steady Performing Champions* and *Explosive Champions*—those who always take everything to a higher-quality level. We need both types in the workplace.

For us to sponsor champions, we must first distinguish between them. If we ask steady performing types to jump over a bar that's set at five feet, they'll do it repeatedly and they won't fail. If we raise the bar, they might make it all the way to six feet. We can't raise the bar too much, however, or we'll set them up for failure.

By contrast, the explosive champions will jump the six feet and clear it by at least two feet. They obviously demonstrate far more natural ability. They're the ones we want to get behind.

The biggest difference between steady performers and the explosive champions is that for Steady Eddies, we have to raise the bar. Explosive champions will raise it for themselves every day. If we can get the steady performing champions to consistently go beyond five feet and encourage them to clear five and a half feet every time, we've increased their capabilities. However, if we consistently ask explosive champions to jump only five and a half feet when they have the ability to scale eight, they become frustrated. Before long they focus their positive abilities elsewhere. That's one major reason we lose some of them.

Some Superman types require more maintenance because of their impatience and desire to raise the bar again. By nature, champions tend to be high maintenance in the *short run*. They require time and resource commitment from their leaders that pays off in the *long run*.

Sponsoring Peers

We live and work in one of the most competitive societies in human history. Even acknowledging that, I want to stress that we have the honor as well as the responsibility to sponsor our *peers*. That isn't easy for everyone to do.

"But what happens if they move ahead of me and I've been here longer?"

"What if they get the dream job I've wanted for three years?"

"What if they get recognized and no one pays any attention to me?"

"Wait a minute! Those are the people I have to compete with every day for recognition, promotions, and opportunities to shine."

All of the statements above are likely to happen!

Sponsoring our peers isn't easy, even though it is the right thing to do. In fact, it seems next to impossible at times, but it's still the right thing to do. Here's why I insist that it's the right thing: It fulfills the second part of Jesus' great commandment. He said the first and greatest was to love God completely and that the second was just as important—to love others in the same way we love ourselves. It's the golden rule of doing for others what we want them to do for us—and even more. It's doing for others whatever we believe God wants us to do.

That applies to our business dealings as well as to peer relationships in our offices. Sponsoring peers seems almost impossible or at best inadvisable—if we listen to other voices. They warn, "If you sponsor a peer, you may lose in the long run."

That's not usually the case. Those who sponsor their peers tend to be as valuable—if not more so—than the peers they get behind. However, politics might rear its ugly head in some organizations.

In the previous chapter I wrote about humility. It's difficult to sponsor peers without that quality. That's because it's next to impossible to use our strengths to bring out the best in others when we're focused on "What's in it for me?" rather than "What's in it for you?"

The most difficult thing about sponsoring peers is that we become afraid—and that also means we're more concerned about ourselves than others and God's will. "What happens if I sponsor him and he gets promoted ahead of me?"

If we're not careful we hold to the law of reciprocity. That is, we expect them to do for us what we did for them. And guess what? They may not reach back and pull us along or recognize our abilities. They may forget they ever knew us. That's the gamble we always take. As those who strive for Unconditional Excellence, we can't base our decisions on how others might respond. We make choices based on what we can do.

Years ago, Jon Ludtke was recruited to work for the Department of Defense as a printer. Jon had a background in printing and came from a family of printers. The recruiter saw something else—the leadership potential. He mentored his protégé. Five years later, Jon became *his* boss.

"You earned this," the man said without any hypocrisy or sense of being wronged because Jon passed him by. He had sponsored a champion and willingly stepped aside when his student surpassed him.

Too many of us would have a hard time admitting, "Bill got

the job I wanted because I sponsored him." We don't want to look foolish or to raise the possibility that we might have sabotaged our own chances at that promotion.

What if Bill deserves the advancement because he's better at his job than I am at mine? What if I strive for excellence, but he's more gifted and efficient than I am? Doesn't he deserve the promotion? Even if Bill politicizes his experience, I still have to trust that God will make everything come out all right in the end. That's part of the burden in believing in a greater power—we have to accept that justice will eventually triumph and that God rewards us for doing the right thing.

I know that; so do most believers. Yet I still have to go home and tell Sara, "I didn't get the new job because I helped Bill get it."

Many of us readily promote our *followers*. We still have authority over them; people expect leaders to take such action. Sponsoring peers, however, is far too uncommon in the business world. When we trounce on our fears and insecurities and actively endorse our peers, think of the effect it produces. Such action sends a message of Unconditional Excellence throughout the entire organization.

Whenever I see an example of peer sponsorship, I know that the person doing the sponsoring has gotten the message. This is the ultimate test—when we're ready to promote someone who may get to march two feet ahead of us. How many of us are willing to go to our bosses and say, "You know, I've been working with Jason for six months. He's too good to be stuck in what he's doing. He's an outstanding worker and you're wasting him where he is."

There can be a downside: Sponsoring peers can become a vehicle for self-promotion. Do you remember the story of Belinda in the previous chapter? When Jenny "helped" the newer worker, she didn't sponsor her—Jenny sponsored Jenny.

That type of scenario goes on all the time in offices. Let's see how the story would have gone if Jenny really sponsored Belinda.

After helping the new worker, Jenny went into Rick's office and said, "I want to tell you that Belinda is an incredibly fast learner. When she struggles with something, she is quick to ask for directions. Let me tell you this much: You have a special worker on your hands."

Rick stops by Belinda's desk and says, "I understand you're a quick learner. I appreciate how you tackle these things and ask those around you to help and support you when you're not sure what to do. You're a good team player, and I think you're doing a great job."

In this fictional scenario, Jenny sponsored Belinda.

When we support our peers in order to receive the credit or to edge toward a promotion for ourselves, we're no longer supporting others. Instead, we're using them for our own gain. Sponsoring peers must be a selfless act. We promote others *because they deserve it*. In the end, it's our trust in that dynamic that ensures we also will benefit.

Doing the Hard Things

Years ago, when I was a sales manager at Pennsylvania House

Furniture, the vice president's position became available in the sales department. I wanted the job, but I didn't pursue it aggressively because it would entail a move from Roswell, Georgia, to Lewisburg, Pennsylvania. Sara and I felt strongly that we wanted our family to have a sense of community right where we were.

We agreed, however, that if the company offered me the position, I wouldn't refuse, because it would eventually lead to the possibility that I could follow my boss up the corporate ladder. He had his eye on a position with the parent company in Chicago, so it was conceivable that within three or four years I could become the CEO.

I didn't engage in politics. Instead of trying to make it known that I was in the running, I waited for my boss to sponsor me. I believed he would, and that took the decision whether to move out of my control.

It turned out that I didn't get the promotion. Instead, my boss chose Tony, a peer manager who was not as good at his job as I was at mine. The other man was political, ambitious, and willing to do whatever it took to get ahead. People who had gotten in his way had heel marks on their backsides as testament to the way he had used them on his climb to the top.

While it may sound like a biased assessment on my part, even our boss shared his concerns about Tony's leadership style and potential as if he were throwing down a challenge before me. The results from his region, while acceptable, were far less than the results from several other regions, including my own. Several of his employees had gone to human resources seeking a transfer to another region and most of his peers expressed open disdain for his political manipulation.

When I heard about the promotion, I complained to the CEO. He shrugged. "You wouldn't move to Lewisburg. He would, so he got the job."

I didn't like that answer. The truth is, I really had wanted that job and the pay increase that went with it. Moving, however, wasn't a sacrifice I was willing to make. As I continued to work at Pennsylvania House, I watched a great company go through turmoil because of poor leadership. Tony wounded people, made many serious business blunders, and had no idea how to stop the company from going downhill. It was as if he were bent on destruction, and all of us who reported directly to him knew we were headed for a serious crisis.

In the three years prior to his promotion, the company had experienced unprecedented growth of over 33 percent annually. Also, our profitability far exceeded the industry norm during this remarkable expansion. Within eighteen months of his taking the job, sales actually began to decline and our remarkable profitability became consistent losses. We went from aggressive and outstanding results to retrenchment within a few years, all as a result of poor leadership.

One night at dinner with the CEO, I asked, "Why are you letting this happen? Why are you allowing him to destroy what so many have built up?"

"Well, it's partly your fault," he said.

"How is it my fault?" I couldn't believe he was trying to put the blame on me. My region was still one of the most productive in the company. We were actually the ones holding the company together.

"You didn't want to take the job."

"What do you mean? I'd have taken the promotion if you had asked me."

He shook his head. "No, Alan. You would have taken the promotion on your terms. Not on the terms I needed it taken."

That remark hurt. "What do you mean by that?"

"You want—you need—everybody to love you. The company had to have change and we had to have someone who could lead the change. I didn't want a person in charge who needed to be liked by everyone. Tony may not be well liked, and maybe he won't do all of the right things, but he'll do the hard things." He paused and stared into my eyes. "You were not willing to do the hard things."

Was that ever a real learning experience for me! He was right. He had tried to sponsor me, but I wasn't ready to be the kind of leader he wanted me to be. I did want—no, I needed— the affirmation of the employees more than I realized. All the while I thought the issue had to do with a willingness to move. In reality, I was saying that I would become a champion only on my own terms.

The sad part was that Tony continued to make a mess of the business. Not only did he do the hard things, he also did many stupid things. I wondered for years if it would have been different if I had been ready to step up the way my old boss wanted me to.

I learned a lot about my own ability to get behind others and challenge them to do the hard things as well as the things they liked. It's easy to sponsor people in the areas they enjoy, but backing them in the areas where they need the most growth is often far more difficult.

For those of us committed to growing into more responsible leadership positions, we need to be willing to do more of the things we must do. As a result, we usually have to sacrifice some of the things we want to do. Sponsoring others only to find out that they aren't willing to pay the price is difficult, especially if we are the ones who end up having to get the hard things done.

Sponsoring the Unlikely

In Chapter 4, I wrote about the dirty job in the furniture factory for sanders and finishers. How do we go about sponsoring sanders? It's an entry-level job involving dirty, terrible work. We knew—and so did they—that none of them were likely to become plant managers. We did have one of them that we could elevate to become supervisor of the sanding line, but what could we do with the rest?

There was only one supervisor on the sanding line. Her name was Deborah. She had been with us for twelve years, loved her work, and declared several times, "I'm going to retire with our company." It wasn't likely that Deborah would leave for several more years. Without any opportunity for those steady champions to advance from the sanding line, what could we do?

It requires growth to create new job openings and leadership opportunities in a company, yet I believed we were heading for a recession. Furniture purchases don't usually make the short list when consumers stop spending. If I had tried to grow the company, I would have put everybody at risk.

As I've stated earlier, when a company isn't experiencing growth and there is virtually no turnover, the result is often that some employees are left with dead-end jobs. People with dead-end jobs can get frustrated with the lack of foreseeable opportunity, and the meaning they find in their work can begin to suffer. How could we use the principle of sponsoring champions for unskilled and semiskilled positions?

Here's what we did. We hired individuals as apprentice sanders where they served for six months. By the end of that period, either they had been promoted to the position of sander or they were not with us any longer. By learning the job and proving they were reliable team players, they earned a promotion.

After two years as a sander, they had the opportunity to become a master sander. We based that title on a number of criteria, including productivity, quality, knowledge of sanding techniques for different woods, and their time/task reliability. Once employees became certified master sanders, they were given a raise of twenty-five cents an hour. They also received a hat with our logo that read *Master*. We put their names in the newsletter and on the master board in the employee break room. Along with their award picture, we also sent the announcement of their achievement to the local newspaper, which always published it.

We made the master sanders responsible for sponsoring each other. That is, the peers became responsible for helping each other grow. They soon developed a strong sense of camaraderie.

Once we had enough master sanders, they became the certification board for the others. The peer review alone increased our productivity and quality.

Since they had to master eleven techniques to become a master sander, those who had already made the grade helped the others progress. If they struggled, say at technique six, a master would say, "Let me show you how I do it." They took more responsibility for making people masters than we did.

The sanders now had meaningful work, better pay, and they had grown in their careers. They were still sanders but they saw growth in their career. They were producing more because for them to become masters they had to maintain a higher productivity level. Every master became a "self-inspected" worker. Thus, quality went up and the need for quality-control supervisors was reduced dramatically.

From time to time we moved people around to six different unskilled production areas and sometimes we had to move people around within those positions. Shipping and receiving was a production area. We had an antiquing process in the production area. There was inventory management control at the front end, and construction was also an area, but sanding and the finishing areas were the two least desirable.

Deborah came up with an idea. After being known as master sanders or master finishers, they could go one step further and become master craftsmen. That happened once they were certified as a master in two of the six production areas in the company.

Besides more money, we also featured them in a section of

our catalog and in our promotional material, with a brief bio on some of the masters. It was unbelievable the impact this program had on the job satisfaction and sense of personal value this created.

That experience taught me a valuable lesson: We can sponsor champions on any level—including unskilled factory workers.

Champions Who Sponsor

I want to tell you about another sponsor of champions. His name is Mike Graham. We met when he was the president of Dittler Brothers, Inc. He had bought a broken company, made it into an excellent organization, and later sold it to a conglomerate.

That sale allowed Mike financial freedom to make important decisions. Over the years I watched him invest in small companies and develop them. For instance, he sponsored a young man named Darren Phelps, who owned a landscaping firm called Divine Designs. It had enormous potential but, like all small companies, it had its difficulties. Darren was capable of producing excellent exclusive designs, but his company didn't yet have the capability to produce the quality of landscaping product that he could design. Darren was the champion, yet his own company could not support his work.

Mike Graham stepped in and sponsored Darren, as well as other individuals in the company. He took over the company, not for any profit motive, but because he saw the potential in each of the people in Divine Designs.

Today Divine Designs is more than ten times larger than it

was. They are rapidly becoming the number one landscaping design firm in the city of Atlanta. They are doing the design work for Stephen Fuller, recognized as one of the premier residential design firms in the country. Darren Phelps had the potential all along. I knew him and saw his work because he did landscaping for our company, but I didn't spot the potential in him.

From Mike Graham, I learned a great deal about sponsoring champions. One valuable lesson was not to set expectations so high that people fail. Set them high enough so that when they succeed they're blown away by their own success, because they didn't know they had it in them.

After Mike took over Divine Designs and made it a company committed to Unconditional Excellence, he changed the lives of everyone who worked for that business. There was no selfish motive in it for Mike. He never asked, "What do I get out of this?"

He took far riskier chances than what I would have taken. In fact, some of us asked, "Why are you doing this?"

"Because I recognize a champion," he said and smiled. "Isn't that neat?"

That's a champion who is committed to sponsoring other champions.

I smiled and wished I had been the one to do that with Darren Phelps.

Competing Motives

Too many of us have been conditioned to compete. We tend to

accept as fact the false logic that if I win, somebody must lose. That is as far from biblical truth as any lie we could possibly believe. We live in a world of competition that conditions us to be just like other people. We're constantly told what we need to do to get ahead; usually, that means we need to self-promote. Therefore, we do just that. In fact, I've had people wonder why I'd even question that concept.

When we're constantly promoting ourselves, we don't get behind each other. How can we? We're so busy trying to win at every opportunity. Yet we could do so much more if we were willing to grasp the concept of mutual interdependence. Cooperation within an organization is what makes teams click. Unconditional Excellence is built on win-win relationships, not win-lose.

Final Sponsoring Words

I want to make it clear that when I refer to sponsoring, I don't mean that we randomly pick people or that we promote those who aren't going to get much out of sponsorship. In a way, we're talent scouts. We seek those who are able and have potential and find ways to help them move forward. We're constantly looking for the as yet undiscovered Clark Kent so we can help make him into Superman. We are also looking for master sanders.

I want to close this chapter with a story about Gary Ivey. Gary exemplifies the concept of sponsoring champions at J. Smith Lanier Company, one of the country's fastest growing and most successful regional insurance brokers. The people he has led and the things he has accomplished along the way testify to his leadership. Gary is a superb recruiter and does intuitively what many of us have to work at.

Over the course of the past ten years, Gary has recruited and sponsored many champions. Their success has been a major reason for J. Smith Lanier's success. What makes Gary unique is that most of these people never knew they were champions—until he came along. Most of them never thought they would grow in their careers and have the impact to the extent they have.

Gary didn't merely see them as they were, but he foresaw the future need and opportunity and recognized the potential in those individuals. Did he make mistakes along the way? Probably, but the organization he heads is dynamic and growing. It's a "Best Place to Work" company because he recruited and then sponsored champions.

At the most recent annual banquet for the company, Gary had the responsibility of awarding the most productive teams their trophies. One by one, as the teams were called forward, Gary would pass them the award, shake their hands, and stand to have his picture taken with them. When one young producer came forward, Gary took a great deal of time whispering to him after he handed him the award. While the photographer waited, I wondered what he was saying.

Later, I asked the young man what Gary told him. He said, "He reminded me that I never dreamed it possible that I could ever achieve the kind of success that I was now realizing. He also reminded me that his greatest joy would be to some day hand me the award that exceeded his own personal achievements. He challenged me to go beyond what he has accomplished and committed to me that he would be there to help me along the way. It really meant a lot for him to take the time to say all that."

chapter twelve

Encouraging
Unconditional Excellence

"I hate to go back to work," Mike Leonard sputtered as he talked about returning to his position at AT&T. "It's so discouraging." That sounded strange to me: Only two weeks earlier, Mike had been full of energy and ebullient as he anticipated an exciting future. The two of us had been given a chance to make our mark and establish ourselves in our careers.

What could have caused such a dramatic turnaround in such a short period?

This experience occurred in the 1980s, as the company was preparing for the breakup of AT&T and the Bell operating companies. The company chose a thousand people from all of the operating companies to take part in a two-week developmental program for sales executives at their training center in Aurora, Colorado. In those days, it was one of the finest training centers in the world.

Before we left, we understood the situation and the odds against us. Our supervisor told us clearly, "Those of you who survive the grueling two-week program will join an elite group of one hundred people who will be fast-tracked for placement within the Bell system."

If we survived, that is—something neither of us chose to focus on. We knew that if we made the final cut, we had our ticket punched for a successful career. If we didn't survive, it didn't mean they would fire or demote us. In fact, before we left for Colorado, the company assured us that we would still have a bright future with Southern Bell in Atlanta (now Bell South). Yes, we all knew that.

For two weeks they put us under the proverbial microscope. They challenged, watched, videotaped, analyzed, and closely scrutinized everything we did. They caught every error, misstep, or hesitation. Every bad presentation became a potential ticket home.

By the end of the first week, five hundred of our peers had washed out. During the second week, the competition got even tougher, and this raised the stakes. While the odds in our favor had doubled—to one in five instead of one in ten—the competition among us increased by a much greater factor. Each of us determined to fight nine or ten times harder to stay in the running.

Every day that we walked into the main room we saw that the numbers were decreasing. Two days before the end of training, Mike Leonard washed out, too.

"I have never felt as depressed as I feel right now," Mike said to me as he packed his bags to return to Atlanta. He had made it down to the final cut. Fewer than two hundred had remained when they cut him—so he had achieved more than eight hundred who had gone home.

Out of the thousand people we started with, on the final

day exactly one hundred of us remained. We were assured that our careers had now been switched to the fast-track program. The other nine hundred—the best of the best from all over the country—were leaving or had already gone. Every one of them was likely just as discouraged as Mike Leonard.

I can understand what the leaders at AT&T were trying to do. They were uncertain of everything about their future except that it would be competitive. To make it worse, most of the people in the company had been raised in a monopolized sales environment. For instance, if we had a difficult customer we often joked that all we had to do was say, "The next time you pick up your phone, listen to the dial tone. If you want to keep that dial tone, just shut up and accept what we have to offer."

Deregulation changed that. An open market required a sales executive team that not only wanted to compete but that had already proven its capability to hold its own. I imagine that was the major reason they made this a pass-fail situation with limited passing slots. One out of ten makes pretty tough odds for success.

While Mike returned home feeling like a loser, I was going home a champion. Not only did I make the cut, but the instructors also voted me the president of the class. It was an honor, and I felt ecstatic. How many times do we get to compete with such high-caliber talent and win the coveted spot? It was a heady experience for me.

At least at first it was.

I kept thinking of Mike and of the others they had sent home. None of them was a loser; none was even mediocre. They still went home feeling rejected and worthless.

The night before our graduation ceremony I hardly slept. Because they had voted me president of the class, my responsibility was to speak to the other ninety-nine members of the group on behalf of my class and then to represent them to the AT&T executives and instructors.

I kept trying to think about what I wanted to say. Perhaps if my friend Mike hadn't been washed out or if he had been able to smile when he left, the experience wouldn't have troubled me so much.

"Mike is a winner," I kept thinking, "but he went home feeling like a loser. That isn't right."

Another troubling factor I kept asking about was this: "Have I let Mike down?" I want to admit that I assumed I would make it and hadn't seriously considered that I might be asked to go home before the course ended. But then, Mike had started with a similar sense of assurance. So had most of the others. Especially during the last three days, when the specter of harsh reality stalked the building, many of them had to face the fact that some were going to make it while others were definitely on the bubble.

The Principle in Action

As crazy as it may sound, I didn't want any of them to be sent home, even though I knew what had to happen. When we first arrived, and without giving it serious thought, I started doing whatever I could to help the others make the grade. I spent most of the nights analyzing other people's presentations, role-playing as a customer, or just listening to their concerns. I felt like a mentor. The experience gave me the opportunity to encourage all those wonderful people and help them to achieve the success they so eagerly sought.

In the process of trying to help others, I learned a great deal. Even more important, I saw the positive effect on what I was trying to do. They didn't treat me as their competitor. More than once, someone said, "You really helped me. I was ready to give up."

One of those who made the final cut hugged me and said, "Without you, I don't think I would have stayed through this. The tension was becoming unbearable, but your confidence in me pushed me through those dark places."

Consequently, when Mike washed out, I felt as if I had some personal responsibility in that. Should I have done more? What if I had given him extra time? Those are unanswerable questions, but they stopped me from having a good night's sleep.

On the final evening, after our instructors had presented the various awards, they announced the final honor—which I already knew was mine—the presidential award. I walked up onto the platform, where everyone expected me to speak for about ten minutes, and I still wasn't sure what to say. I had rehearsed a few things, but they lacked the power of conviction. They were words I thought I should say to please my peers and the executives, but none of my comments held much passion.

I wish I had a tape of that short talk. It was perhaps one of my best, even though it certainly wasn't the most prepared or eloquent. Here is the gist of it:

"First, I want to thank my boss, Tony Key back in Atlanta, for nominating me for this program. Tony is a man who recognizes ability and brings out the best in others. He's a great asset to this company." I meant that about Tony. He was always looking for people to sponsor, people he could promote. I had been one of them and I was immensely grateful.

"I'd also like to thank all the instructors who gave so much of their time, energy, and experience to help us succeed." Even as I spoke, I realized that those words didn't apply to the other nine hundred of us who had already left for home. When they walked into their home offices, everyone would have known immediately that they had failed to make the cut. What a contrast from the time when they'd left for Aurora, when others had rallied behind them as the best and brightest. In two short weeks their lights were significantly dimmer and their confidence significantly diminished.

"I have learned something here in Aurora that is much more valuable than the content of the material we have studied. For the past two weeks I have watched my peers drop like flies in the heat of competition. For the past week, our wing of the training center has looked and sounded like a dorm during finals. Never have I seen so many people so committed to succeed than during this last week. Yet many of them have gone home feeling like failures. I wish they could have heard a few words of praise. I wish they could have known that we realize they gave their best, and they deserve credit for trying. I wish they could have shared in this moment with me."

At this point, I held up a marker that a previous speaker had left on the lectern. I walked to the front of the platform and held the marker above my head. I dropped it to the floor and returned to the lectern.

"Just as much as we believe in gravity—the gravity that caused that marker to drop—I believe there is another principle at work. That's the reason I am up here. Here is the principle: When we give away anything good, and when we do it for the benefit of others, it is returned to us. More than that, it is multiplied. Last week I thought I gave encouragement away to people who needed it desperately, to some of you in this room and to many who did not make it.

"Jesus once said that if we give, we would receive, and that what we received would be given to us in an even greater measure than the amount we gave. I believe those words and want to live by them.

"I gave to the others here—and I'm pleased to say that what I got in return was far more valuable. The more I gave it away, the more I had to give. The more I thought I was helping, the more I was helped. The more I gave, the more I received.

"I hope we all learned some of that lesson this week, because for us to be truly successful over the next few years, we are going to need a lot of courage and we're going to need to rally behind others."

I paused and looked over the audience before I said, "I wish my friend Mike Leonard was here. He would be greatly encouraged by all of this and our company needs to find ways to hearten and reassure our Mike Leonards if we are to compete successfully."

Gift, or Learned Ability?

I hadn't made a particularly stirring or politically satisfying speech, but I did get across the things that I needed to say. What was important to me was that I discovered something about myself—something that would change my life and guide the way I dealt with others in the future.

This was one of those *"Aha!"* moments when I realized the importance of the power of encouragement. I knew intuitively that the one thing we can offer others is to inspire and lift them up, especially when they are rolling around in pain, defeat, or discouragement. I also realized that God had given me a gift—a special gift—to encourage others.

I call it a gift because it wasn't something I had to figure out, plan for, or manipulate circumstances in order to use. I simply did it. That's important to point out. In this chapter, I stress the importance of encouraging others. Some of us do that naturally and easily and may not even be aware that we're gifted that way.

Others may have to cultivate this ability. They may have to think about it and look for ways to sincerely hearten others. I believe that is my greatest contribution to the scheme of things.

Encouragement Defined

When I define *encouragement*, I like to think of it as "filling with courage." Earlier in this book I told about Feet Motley. During the time we spent together I tried to do just that. As I tried to instill courage in him, my own heart was filled. I also know he gave away as much as I gave him because Feet became an unmitigated cheerleader for his peers.

That's a success story for me. By contrast, I regret the many times I thought employees, bosses, and coworkers wanted some profound insight, answers to pressing problems, or for me to make key decisions on matters of great importance. In most of those instances, many of them just needed assurance—the kind that comes from outside them—that word that makes them know they can succeed. They needed to know that I was with them, supporting them and caring about them, and that I would do whatever I could to make them look good.

The business world is tough and competitive enough when things are going well. When business is cycling downward—especially when the owners expected it to cycle upward—the atmosphere can be downright hostile and destructive. That's when we need more encouragers, especially those of us who can reach out and assure others they can attain Unconditional Excellence. We need to infuse others with confidence as much as we need to receive it from others; nobody can make his or her way alone.

When We Need Encouragement

When do employees—and employers—most need encouragement? When do they need those words and gestures that rally their spirits and pull them out of despair? Is it

- When our business soars?
- When we're all hitting our numbers?
- When the economy is booming?
- When the projections look great?
- When our biggest competitors have gone out of business to leave their market share for us?

Of course not! The answer is that we need someone to lift us up when we're afraid, depressed, worn out, or burning out. We need encouragement when the economy is tanking but our sales are dropping. We need to be filled with courage when most of us have nothing left to give.

Too many leaders believe encouragement means a pat on the back for a job well done, an "'Atta boy" for completing a task, or a bonus at the end of the year. Let's call that recognition rather than encouragement.

Although I believe recognition is one of the most inexpensive but effective motivators we have as leaders, I do not believe it has the power of encouragement.

Characteristics of Encouragers

Rick Stroud is one of my crisis heroes. When all hell is breaking loose, Rick stands firm. Over the years I have watched him lead in the midst of calamity and seen the impact he has had on people who probably never thought they could survive. But they did—and largely because Rick helped them believe they could. He is an encourager of the highest degree, even though on the surface he appears to be a quiet, reserved leader.

Hope

Another common trait encouragers exhibit is what the Bible calls hope. When the Bible uses *hope* (from the Greek, *elpizo,* which means hope in its active, verbal sense), it does not mean to express a vague wish, daydream, or desire. Biblical hope is much stronger. It conveys the sense of expectation, confidence, or assurance of results. Hope believes that conditions will get better, situations will improve, or that circumstances will work out for good. Not a blind optimism, hope clearly sees all of the obstacles but chooses to believe in the positive outcome, in spite of those obstacles. Hope is able to focus ahead and envision the positive and possible results that haven't yet been achieved. Those who embody this sense of hope also have the innate ability to pass it on to others and to infuse them with the same sense of expectation.

Previously, I mentioned Dale Bissonette, the CFO of S. D. Myers and Company. Dale is full of this high caliber of hope, which he readily dispenses to others even though I'm not sure he realizes how much he affects others.

Dale in his turn has been greatly impacted by Chuck Baker, the best example I know. The two of them together have created a culture of hope and encouragement at Myers. They have profoundly influenced that environment as they continue to build a company of Unconditional Excellence.

Discernment and Wisdom

These two are different concepts, but we can't separate them in the matter of encouragement. They are like opposite sides of the same quality. Encouragers need to be able to see the need for them to use their ability—and that requires discernment. But to be fully effective they also need to offer a solution, and that takes wisdom. (The solution may be only the next step for the person to take to pull out of despair and not necessarily the final answer.)

I have a good friend and business associate, Mike Graham, who is an encourager to me and who embodies both discernment and wisdom. Mike can address the heart of an issue because he cuts through all extraneous issues to the heart of conflict or the need. He provides wise counsel in matters because he sees beyond the problem straight to the solution. Too many people can define the dilemma for me, but unless they have something to offer in the way of solutions, they haven't helped me very much. I know many consultants who make their living by pointing out problems. The best make a better living by pointing out answers and then inspiring others to apply them.

My experiences convince me that the ability to encourage is a more powerful tool than we give it credit for being. I also contend that, if we were to place a greater emphasis on this single quality, it could change the culture of any organization as dramatically as any of the other applied skills or principles. I believe this so strongly that I consider it one of the critical roles of Unconditional Excellence in leadership.

If encouragement is important for positional leaders, isn't

it just as important for employees who lead through their character and competence authority?

Every successful CEO that I admire in the business world has the gift of encouragement. It's part of what made them who they are, as both leaders and guides of an organization's present and future.

The role of the encourager was a major gift General George C. Patton gave soldiers during World War II. Most people recognized this quality in Ronald Reagan during his two terms in office. Mother Theresa modeled encouragement to outcasts in Calcutta and others she encountered around the world. The world's greatest encourager was Jesus Christ, who promised his followers that he would be with them all through their lives. Regardless of your political bent, no one exhibited this incredible skill more than Mayor Rudy Guiliani of New York City. After September 11th, 2001, he became America's most beloved mayor and an encouragement to an entire world.

Every one of us, no matter what our status in an organization, also has the potential to become a great encourager. Most of us need a hand to lift us up at some time during our careers, especially in the middle of great difficulty or crisis. When a leader has the ability to inspire and make others more confident, the doors are often opened for us to take additional steps up the ladder of success.

Most leaders intuitively recognize which employees have this gift. They're those who come through when deadlines draw near. They're the ones to whom we might say, "You're my model. My hero," even if they are coworkers or someone who ranks below us in the company. No matter how discouraging the news, they're the ones who say, "Now that we know the worst, we know we don't have to give up. We can make it."

Who Encourages Whom?

It's easy to see the scenario of the struggling receptionist or computer programmer who needs a word of hope. It's normal to look at those around us or those who are lower on the economic ladder. It is unfortunate, however, that many of us miss seeing an immensely needy group of people who want us to strengthen them: *They are those who lead us.*

I'm convinced that one of the greatest needs in the corporate world is for our leaders to receive encouragement from the people they lead. Team leaders need the approbation and support of the teams they lead. It takes a never-ending supply of courage to lead people in business today to Unconditional Excellence, especially during difficult economic times.

Practical Encouragement

Would you do something right now? It's a simple exercise that you can do in less than two minutes.

Step One

Close your eyes and think about the people you work with or have worked with in the past. Which individuals make your day brighter? Who helps you understand that your contribution counts? Who makes you feel that you have something to contribute?

Step Two

Ask yourself, "Why?" Why are they encouragers? Why do they do it? Why do I feel stronger and more affirmed after I have been in their presence? I'm not only referring to people who make you feel good, such as the jokesters or funny people, but those individuals who fill you with courage and who make you know that you are not going to fail.

Step Three

Ask yourself, "What qualities do they have that make them stand out from the crowd? What do they say or do that strengthens me to strive for Unconditional Excellence?"

Step Four

Why not commit yourself to learn from their example? Why not decide that you will cultivate the ability to affirm others as you have been affirmed?

Final Step

Go to your boss, supervisor, or manager, just to encourage him or her. Consider the obstacles the company faces and the pressures that person is under every day. Assure your boss that he or she can continue rising above the daunting problems. Share your *hope* that things will be better. It may also be that when you offer your support, you may be able to give that person a word of wisdom.

As you did this simple exercise, the people you thought of are probably those who respond well to crisis. While the rest of the office panics, they consider before they react. People with that special ability see crisis as an opportunity to bring out the best in others. Because it is often during a crisis that we need the uplift from others, that's when the gifted people come through best.

It takes little to lift up others. Even leaders need caring, committed followers behind them—the kind that cheer them on as they lead the parade.

Here is an added bonus. If you do what I suggest, when you leave that person you've encouraged, you will also stand a little taller and be more assured than you were before you reached out.

That's how encouragement operates. You can't give without receiving. The only way to truly lose all of your own hope and courage is to never share it.

One of the men I admire and respect the most in the business world is J. Smith Lanier, chairman and CEO of the brokerage firm J. Smith Lanier. Smith is no longer active in the day-to-day business, but he keeps his office in West Point, Georgia, and maintains regular contact with people in the agency.

He said something to me that I consider to be one of the greatest rewards of my call to Unconditional Excellence. "You must have been talking to some of our people," Smith said, smiling as only he can. When Smith smiles, even the sun gets a little brighter. "Two people came into my office last week to encourage me and to thank me for giving them the opportunity to work at our agency."

Smith beamed as he said, "I couldn't think of a better reward than what those two women shared with me. It makes all of the effort, all of the challenges, and all of the work worthwhile."

I beamed. He was encouraged. I was encouraged. The two women were encouraged. How powerful and meaningful were those few words, yet too often we fail to speak them because we don't think it will make a difference. Trust me; it will. Try it. You will be glad you did.

When Smith told me, I was actually surprised—surprised that only *two* employees had gone to him. However, I later learned at least ten people had gone to Gaines Lanier, who is now the president. Gaines is also a man I admire greatly for his commitment to the same principles as his uncle, Smith, and exemplifies the same passion for leaving behind a great legacy. Gaines took what Smith handed him and has made it even better.

Maybe you are not up to a visit with your boss, or it might be that you have nothing encouraging to share. In that case, consider sharing courage with a peer or coworker. Start today. Look around you. I'm sure—right where you work—there are people who need an infusion of courage right now. The working world can be a cruel, harsh, and scary place. People need someone to bring them rays of hope and glimmers of sunshine. You might be just the person.

Who knows? You might make an important difference in the life of a coworker in the next cubicle or at the desk next to yours. It is one of the easiest first steps to make on this journey called Unconditional Excellence, and it is well worth the effort.

chapter thirteen

Peacemakers

When I was working on the content of the seminar that eventually became this book, I struggled about whether to use the word *peacemaking* instead of *conflict resolution*. Peacemaking sounds like a religious word, one that doesn't quite fit the tension and tumult of the marketplace. We think of peacemakers as people who wander around monasteries, deep in thought, blessing and smiling at everyone as they pass by.

The term may sound soft and unworldly, but it isn't. I have come to appreciate this concept to such a degree that I would even go so far as to say that peacemakers are possibly the most valuable workers we have in the workplace today.

But before we examine this skill—and it is a skill—let's examine its opposite.

Conflict Makers

"Conflict is a necessary ingredient for any successful company," Ed Roberts said. He was then my boss, a man who thrived on disputes and disagreements. If we didn't have a controversy, he'd create it. Ed believed that tension created an environment that brought the best out in champions. He also thought that surviving such skirmishes made us better leaders and more productive. Ed was a top conflict maker.

I have met so many leaders who believe the same as Ed Roberts that I suspect there must be a business course or a book somewhere that teaches disruption as a vital part of organization. Some people, like Ed, make an art form of such clashes.

Regardless, it isn't right. Disharmony and disagreements create negative energy, which is a waste: The energy needed to resolve crises could otherwise be directed positively and for greater accomplishments. The negativity destroys the fiber of community, humility, integrity, and Unconditional Excellence.

Ed Roberts epitomizes what I consider a deliberate conflict maker. He set people up in competitive situations, where everyone became either a winner or a loser. He made certain everyone knew that "to the victor belongs the spoils." What happens in such environments?

Politics happen and relationships are destroyed. Trust becomes a negotiable commodity. People create schisms and build silos to defend themselves against such battles.

Some leaders, like Ed, are unabashedly proud of the negative differences they produce because they can point to the outcomes (usually short-term), and say, "See. That happened as a result of the controversy I set up. We win because the winners win." Forgetting what happens to the losers is easy for the Eds of the world because they consider the losers in the combat to be just that—losers.

There is another large group of individuals whose influence is not as deliberate as Ed's, but they are potentially just as destructive. We know them as the workplace politicians. With no disrespect intended toward professional, elected public servants, this common term describes those within an organization who seem to believe that by creating disruption, they will end up on the positive side of the outcome.

There are three political types we need to be leery of: *rumormongers, dung kickers, and dissension sowers.*

Don't think for a minute that I haven't practiced and participated in all of these things. I have. Most likely, so has everyone else at some time. Once we recognize the negativity they produce, we can crusade to wipe them out.

Rumormongers

They love to be at the center of the buzz. Truth is usually irrelevant because gossip is far juicier.

Those who spread such gossip flourish because passing on news that others don't know affirms them. Rumormongers believe people consider them on the inside—those "in the know."

Rumormongers are weak and insecure, and spreading rumors is one device that allows them—momentarily at least—to feel better about themselves. I suspect that rumormongers fear that they will be found out, so they keep the attention focused on others instead. For some, it's their way of gaining attention or favor, failing to grasp that people never really trust them because of their desire to share unfounded stories and gossip.

Even though we realize (if we think about it) that we may

become the object of such gossip, all too often we listen to the gossip mill. We think we can separate rumors from the facts. What we do by listening is to feed the discord.

Unconditional Excellence requires not only that we avoid any participation in rumors and gossip, but that we become the fire hose that extinguishes the flame. It takes a lot of personal courage to tell a rumormonger, "That's enough. Stop. I really don't want to hear and I would expect you to stop spreading it." You won't be popular, but you will be respected and trusted.

Shirley Murphey, an employee of a publishing firm, did just that. When a coworker began gossiping about a colleague she said, "Please don't. Ruth is my friend and I don't want to hear anything bad about her."

Dung Kickers

These people are similar to rumormongers, but they are more insidious. I have no idea why they do what they do, but I have met far too many dung kickers in my career. I want to shine the light on them so we can see them for what they are.

The dung kicker doesn't create the problems. But like a kid on the farm, they'll kick a pile of dung just to stir up the flies. They're also the kind who throws gasoline on a fire rather than trying to put it out.

- "I'm sure you're not going to like this, but Susanne was in Larry's office this morning. They were talking about you."
- "You shouldn't let him do that to you. You should call in sick and let them figure out if you really are or not."

- "Isn't it sad that Mary uses her relationship with Bill to get the best assignments and you get stuck with the junk? Maybe you should go and talk to Edna about this. Believe me, she's got Mary's number."

We've heard them all. The worst ones come across as sweet, compassionate, concerned, and even helpful, yet in reality they are poison. Dung kickers are either trying to draw attention away from themselves because they feel so poorly about themselves or they are trying to create a situation that looks bad to make their situation look good by comparison.

Dissension Sowers

Dung kickers and rumormongers don't just create clashes—they help spread the fire and fan the flames. Dissension sowers, however, create the situations and allow the others to add fuel that makes their work effective. Of the three, they're the most destructive and their motives are usually very clear. They want to gain advantage, to draw attention away from themselves, undermine others—usually perceived competitors—or to be recognized as an expert who can put out the fire, without letting anyone realize they started it in the first place.

The first role of the peacemaker is to identify these human conflict-makers and thwart their ability to create, stir up, or spread dissension. The most difficult peacemaking role is the one that confronts a boss who wrongly insists that dissension is a good thing. In many of these situations, the sensible response is usually to remove ourselves from the source by transferring to another department or leaving the company.

At this writing, I'm dealing with a business where three of the conflict-makers are working together to create a hellish situation for the rest of the employees. Their CEO believes—wrongly—that infighting is good for the company; he may not have directly created the dissension of the past three years, but he has certainly allowed it. The vice president of sales and marketing is essentially retired. With just a year left on his contract, he does everything he can to stir up controversy in other areas of the business, particularly in operations, so that the focus will be on them and not on the fact that he has a short-termer's work pattern.

Another leader within operations is a rumormonger, always careful to add, "Well, I didn't hear him say it *directly* but I understand John told Alice that he . . . " What a mess.

This week I sat down with the CEO and helped him understand that he needs to address the areas of disharmony he has helped to create. He also needs to re-establish trust throughout the organization. I believe he'll be able to make the change.

As for the others, we have scheduled a leadership summit. I have called each of them individually and said, "Be prepared to talk openly and honestly about any subject we need to address to clear the air and move forward. If you can't say it publicly, I want to know why right now. Speak next week, or forever hold your peace." No one said anything.

At that summit I will establish a code of conduct that shuts off the source of politics. They may, of course, try to take he clashes underground. I hope not. I also hope that the overall quality of leadership and commitment to Unconditional

Excellence they have made will make a positive difference and spread harmony and trust.

The great discovery for me was that peacemakers already existed within this leadership team. Those gifted team members are aggressively and boldly committed to ending the controversy.

Enemy at the Gates

Despite the many conflict-makers inside our organizations, for our purposes let's consider that they come from external sources, circumstances, and situations. Because of the nature of competition, the business world will always exist under a cloud of potential discord.

- Our best supplier takes proprietary information and gives it to our competition so he can gain a little more business. That creates conflict.
- Our major competitor is going out of business so they drop their prices to below what it costs us to make our product because they want to liquidate inventory and pay off debt. That creates conflict.
- Our employees have decided that the union message is just too good to pass up, so they have called for an organizing vote. That creates conflict.

The list seems endless. It is this kind of trouble that mediators were made for, because at the core of their being, they're the best warriors any business can have. This points out why peacemaking isn't a weak, pious role but a task for those with character and a desire for Unconditional Excellence.

Competition versus Conflict

I would be remiss if I didn't address another potential source of tension—competition. There are two ways for me to win a race. The first is to run my very best and make sure I run faster than anyone else. The second way is to trip anyone who tries to pass me. We trip others by jealousy, envy, mean-spiritedness, and in hundreds of subtle ways. No matter what we do, our methods come down to a lack of integrity and humility. Covenantal relationships are those that stand firm, even under the harsh glare of competition. We must be able to compete without arousing controversy.

Here's one of those stories that I love to tell because it makes my point. Two men are hiking through the woods when they spot a large, angry grizzly bear coming their way. They know they can't get away from it. Just before they make a break for it, one of them stops, opens his backpack, removes a pair of running shoes, and hurries to put them on.

The other man scoffs, "Are you nuts? You can't outrun a grizzly bear."

" I don't have to," he replied. "I just need to outrun you."

Too often that's our attitude, isn't it?

Ed Roberts was the master at setting up competitive situations that had only one winner; thus, he created one skirmish after another. Because of the nature of business, we'll always have to deal with competition. If we grasp the character skills presented earlier, it becomes easier to compete with excellence without destroying others. That has to be particularly true when we strive for recognition, promotions, or pay increases.

The answer to this dilemma lies in a simple concept called cooperative competition. In a previous chapter I wrote about Mike Leonard and the AT&T training center in Colorado, one of the best examples I know of cooperative competition. I learned the principle by first living it. I helped a number of other men in a situation where all of us knew that only one hundred would be chosen from the field of a thousand wannabes.

Since that ordeal, I've realized that we win whenever we do everything we can to bring out the best in others—including our competition. Even if they win, we also win under this principle. If the only way for me to win is for someone else to lose, Unconditional Excellence would have little appeal.

The Power of Peacemaking

In the midst of fighting, the power to live a peacemaker's life reveals Unconditional Excellence more clearly than anything else we can do. Whether the issues involve us personally or whether we see discord around us, we are called to build relationships by being peacemakers.

We don't have to be so afraid of discord, however, that we don't grasp the potential that conflict creates for developing stronger and more committed relationships. Good, healthy connections don't only grow in the garden of plenty; they can also flourish in the valley of dissent and disharmony—if we're committed to nurturing those affiliations. Most marriages I know don't have their best growth when everything runs smoothly; the times when two people face the struggles of paying their bills, managing their careers, and raising a family strengthens them and their relationship.

The best relationships I've had in the business world grew out of the times when we had to come together to resolve issues. It is one of those "aligned to a common goal" principles that make for great teams and true bonding.

We also need to be aware that controversy can break a connection. In the workplace, the way we handle our differences determines whether we strengthen or ruin the relationship. That means that when we accept the role of peacemakers, we have a thrilling opportunity to bring harmony on the job. Given the high potential for disputes and antagonism at work, we will probably have a long and fruitful career if we can be the peacemakers.

To be a powerful peacemaker we need the skills to:

- Do everything in our power to anticipate differences before they appear; therefore, we avoid them.
- Analyze the source of the dissension, then separate symptoms and circumstances from problems.
- Aggressively address the dispute as if enemies were threatening everything we hold dear.

The Core of Conflicts

To develop the skills to avoid, analyze, and address discord, we need to understand what lies at the core of the issues. For the conflict-makers, the center is clearly wrong beliefs about controversy or a flaw in their character. (Of course, there are far more reasons that serious differences arise than those I've mentioned.)

Ken Sandy probably knows more about peacemaking than I'll ever know. I've learned from him and many of my ideas came from him. He wrote *The Peacemaker: A Biblical Guide to Resolving Personal Conflict.*[2] Ken is the president of Peacemakers International, a conflict-resolution ministry.

Ken says there are three real major reasons serious differences arise:

1. Lack of Humility

Everything revolves around me, my, and mine. We live in a my-rights generation among those who ask, "What's in it for me?" As long as we focus on ourselves, we'll always have disharmony.

2. Lack of Alignment

People are at variance because they don't know where they're going. Either they think they're in agreement with others, or they don't take seriously the minor issues that separate them. (See Chapter 5.)

---

[2]Sandy, Ken. *The Peacemaker: A Biblical Guide to Resolving Personal Conflict.* (Grand Rapids, MI: Baker Book House, 1997).

3. Lack of Good Communications

Too often we discover this lack after contention has erupted.

"I thought your memo meant—"

"But you said that—"

"I didn't understand you meant that—"

"That was urgent? Your voice mail didn't sound—"

Any of these three causes has the potential to cause all kinds of disaster. This is especially significant when we have all three together—those without humility, those without alignment, mixed with people who don't communicate well.

What is the best way to avoid or resolve disharmony? Simply deal with the problems that create discord rather then chasing the symptoms and circumstances. Previous chapters on problem solving outlined the process for developing Unconditionally Excellent problem-solving skills. They are peacemaking skills as well.

Since communication problems lie at the core of many issues, developing Unconditional Excellence in communications is essential. Misalignment is another core source of trouble; it's therefore critical to create alignment personally and then align with the corporate or organizational goals and objectives to help bring about alignment.

Self-centeredness or self-interest is another basic cause. Only by living a covenantal life, modeling humility, and sponsoring others will we be effective mediators.

Each of the competency skills and character skills I've already presented are parts of a greater whole. Individually, they are powerful. When collectively applied, they define Unconditional Excellence. Nowhere is that more evident than when we become intermediaries in a culture desperately needing to see the face of God.

In his most famous teaching—the Sermon on the Mount—Jesus Christ boldly declared a blessing on the peacemakers and said they would see the face of God. While I don't fully understand how that works, I readily accept the truth that it reveals. I have also seen how peacemakers become the ones who themselves reveal the face of God to those in turmoil.

Teams and the Conflict Within

Teaming is an effective way to avoid, analyze, and aggressively deal with controversy, yet all too often our issues within the team lead to greater problems when the teams don't work well. Teams provide circumstances and environments that have potential for creating discord, so we must always be vigilant to avoid it at all costs.

In fact, from my perspective, *the* single most important individual on any team is the peacemaker. That person is often more essential than the leader because that influence can work through the entire team. The arbitrator is the person who glues everyone together.

This is a vital role for successful teamwork; it's also the most difficult. Peacemakers have to earn the respect of the others. Because peacemakers are supportive of everyone and try not to uplift one person or faction, others don't always understand them immediately. People often don't trust them, and frequently they're suspected of doing things for their own advantage.

As long as the leader is not a conflict-maker, peacemakers thrive in a team environment. Teams where everyone is skilled at appeasing in healthy ways will produce consistently outstanding results, develop strong and lasting relationships, and create a cooperative, competitive culture that brings out the best in everyone. The collective brilliance of a team is brightest when the individuals are committed peacemakers, regardless of the task the team is trying to accomplish.

The Anatomy of a Conflict

Years ago, I discovered that there are five stages in the development of conflict.

First Stage: Defend Our Position

At this point nothing is personal; we're just in disagreement, or are misaligned with, someone else's viewpoint. Consider how often we have heard customer service reps say, "Well, our policy is . . . and that is why we can't handle it the way you would like."

While it is okay and often necessary to defend a correct position, it does begin the process of building up defenses. What would happen if our first responsibility were to understand the other person's position? Might it help avoid disruption or quickly resolve it once it begins?

Yes. Definitely, yes.

Second Stage: Attack the Other Person's Position

"I am sorry that the product is broken, but you should have dealt with the shipper before you contacted us. This sounds like a freight problem, not a quality problem, and you need to handle it with your freight carrier first."

Now, both of us are beginning to heat up. Voices grow a little louder; hearts beat a little faster. The lines of engagement are being drawn. If I am going to have to defend my position, the easiest way is to attack the enemy's defenses. Pat MacMillan called it the "hardening of the categories" when we clog the communication arteries with discord and antagonism.

Third Stage: Attack the Person

Once emotions are on edge, we move to the next stage. This is where one of them yells something like:

- "I can't believe your attitude."
- "Sir, you seem to have a problem dealing with issues without getting upset."
- "You really have a temper problem, don't you?"
- "You never get it done on time."
- "You seem to have constant problems with situations like this."
- "I can't believe you actually understand what you just said. Are you dense or something?"
- "Keep this up, and I'll show you what a battle looks like."

Sometimes we're more subtle, but it's still a personal attack.

Fourth Stage: Attack Our Enemies When They Aren't Looking

This happens when we have a small audience and the other person isn't around.

- "Doesn't it drive you nuts when she does that? How can you put up with her?"
- "I am amazed that he can get away with so much and that he flaunts it right under your nose, boss."
- "I can tell you this: If you sent her over to our department, we'd take *care* of her attitude problem real quickly."

Fifth Stage: Build Permanent Emotional Barriers

Even after we have resolved our differences, we maintain the blockades of unforgiveness, lack of trust, and open hostility. This situation also leads to a destructive culture because we sacrifice Unconditional Excellence for conditional enmity.

Anatomy of a Resolution

The best way to avoid the downward spiral is to see the conflict from the other perspective first. Even if we must maintain our position, it is still more effective to start from the other side than to dig foxholes on our side of the battle line.

First: Shift Our Thinking

We have to do it before we defend our position. By the time we have begun to defend, it's too late. As soon as we're aware of discord, we need to pull back and consider the other's perspective. That doesn't mean compromise or giving up, but it does mean being open-minded.

Outstanding sales people know that one of the simplest selling techniques is to restate the buyer's objectives and desires before presenting a solution. Instead of putting the buyer on the defensive, we gain by nodding positively in agreement. That person then knows we have been listening. With a simple gesture, we have begun to move toward a "yes" from our buyer.

That's exactly the first principle in being a peacemaker. If we understand the other's viewpoint, *our defenses* are down. We're ready to agree. In conflict, too often we attempt to do the opposite and our goal then shifts to resolving the differences.

Second: Start at the End and Move Backward

By that, I mean we first need to figure out the conclusion. What do we want to accomplish? What is the desired result?

This may sound obvious, but too often we find ourselves in skirmishes because we focus on the means to get to the end instead of concentrating on the end we want to achieve. Then, because of misalignment and bad communication, we never get to the end because we become bogged down with words and defending our positions.

We take a major step toward resolving differences if we say: "If we accomplished . . . then would you be satisfied?" Or

"If we agreed on . . . would that solve your problem?"

Suppose we were to say to the customer, "If you were able to keep the product and pay only the original invoice and not the additional handling charges, would that solve the problem?" If the answer is yes when the original position was, "I want to return everything," we now have a clear resolution in sight. Once we have agreed on what it should look like at the end, it is significantly easier to resolve the conditions that keep us from reaching that end alignment.

Suppose the credit manager protests, "Our policy is not to give credit for handling charges because the salespeople are taught to tell customers they must pay them."

I regularly heard those words from the credit manager in my earliest days in the furniture business. He would hold up hundreds of thousands of dollars of invoices over a few hundred dollars in handling charges. Naturally, that attitude infuriated dealers and angered sales reps. The company I represented developed a poor reputation because we were seen as inflexible and difficult business partners.

I'll bet that sounds familiar. It is at epidemic proportions right now in customer service departments in businesses around the globe. We call it bad customer service, but it's really poor conflict resolution. Often it's our policies that create much of the problem, because they put people in situations where the natural outcome will produce disagreement. Then we wonder why we have so much disharmony.

Once we know more about conflict, we become better equipped for peacemaking. The best peacemakers scan the horizon, detect potential problems, and use all of their skills to keep those potential problems from becoming real problems.

To be an effective arbitrator takes initiative. In cases where being an arbitrator is imperative, we use another of the Unconditionally Excellent skills.

If we can't avoid disputes—and there are times we can't— we use our best problem-solving skills to analyze and separate the problem from the symptom or circumstance.

Finally: Use Personal Strengths to Create Harmony

This is evidenced by mutually beneficial resolution, as we aggressively use our best tools to bring harmony. As we do so, we need to make certain we align with a mutually beneficial resolution. We need to face conflict-makers who constantly cause or stir up discord because of self-interest or a lack of character and commitment.

By communicating with Unconditional Excellence, we either avoid such skirmishes entirely or face them constructively if they do arise.

Here's my version of Jesus' blessing for those who disarm the warriors and bring harmony out of chaos: "Blessed are the peacemakers, for they make life better for all of us."

chapter fourteen
Aiming High

When I first began teaching Unconditional Excellence, I was reluctant to draw too much attention to the source, which is God's wisdom. I didn't want these principles to get confused with the negative, checklist mentality that pervades some religious teachings. These principles work in every aspect of the market-place. God's isn't in the "don't-do" business.

Raising the Bar

Instead of the "don'ts," Unconditional Excellence needs to be defined by the "do's" of the spiritual life. If you can learn to think that way, you won't lower your expectations and your standards. You'll set and attain higher levels. When you raise the bar, you aim higher and stretch yourself beyond your comfort zone. You venture into areas where too few go—the realm of Unconditional Excellence.

This is definitely a "road less traveled" experience, because too many are comfortable and complacent in aiming low. It's like handling competition by tripping others rather than encouraging them to run their best and racing the best we can at the same time.

You can achieve Unconditional Excellence only if you aim high, jump over the bar, and raise the bar again. Unconditional Excellence means a constant raising of your sights throughout the course of your life.

Every skill I've presented allows for your growth. In fact, every one is a skill that you can get better at over time. For instance, my ability to communicate today is far better than when I was just out of college. If you aren't raising your sights, you miss so much of the good life that God wants you to have.

"What's Love Got to Do with It?"

Possibly the most rewarding experience I've ever had in business was when the president and CEO of J. Smith Lanier and Company, Gaines Lanier, opened a leadership meeting by saying, "It's really all about serving people by loving people. We have to make active decisions to love others every day." This from one of the most dynamic, effective, and excellent leaders I know. It is all about unconditional love.

I agree, even though that's not the kind of language we usually hear in the marketplace. Years ago, Tina Turner's hit song asked, "What's Love Got to Do with It?" It is also a great question to ponder. Is there a place for unconditional love in the business world?

"The business world isn't about love," I can hear the scoffers say. "It's all about profit, performance, and competition."

They are absolutely wrong. We serve people by loving people. Isn't that the greatest untapped motivator we have at our disposal as we seek to maximize productivity, performance, and profitability, *learning how to value people by loving them?* I use the word *love*, although some might prefer to substitute *care* in the marketplace. The concept is valid no matter what we call it.

Loving isn't accepting mediocrity or becoming a softie that tolerates everything.

Assisting others as they attain their highest personal standards is more loving than accepting their failures with a few well-meaning platitudes.

Think of it this way:

> If I make a commitment to seek the best in others, and if I use my natural and developed abilities to bring out the best in others, then we can accomplish worthwhile things together. Isn't that following the example of Jesus?

Loving also means caring enough to challenge others to set and attain the highest standards.

A tenet of the Christian faith and most other religions states that in the end, we must give an account of what we did with our lives. Here's one way to face the answer. We ask ourselves: Did my life count for something more meaningful than a financial statement? Or try this question: Is there a better way to make our lives count than putting high value on people—that is, by loving them? I don't think so.

Why are we afraid of using the word *love* in business relationships? Is it because we don't understand what it really means? Is it because we think love is something we leave at the church door on Sunday? After all, we don't want it to get in the way of our priorities on Monday and disrupt business. Isn't it just possible that our business world would go more smoothly and that we'd be more content if we used love as our motivator?

The Story of Bess

I want to share a true story about Bess, who exemplifies motivating love in action. Bess is too modest to allow me to use her real name. She's a woman who quietly lived all the principles I've referred to in this book. I could sum it all up by saying that she quietly lived by the principle of love. She wasn't the CEO or division manager. In fact, I don't believe she ever held a position of leadership in all her career. I met Bess when I was taking her company through the seminar that this book is based on. Very quickly I realized that Bess epitomizes Unconditional Excellence.

Bess is nearing the end of her career, having served her company for more than twenty years. Throughout all those years, she has modeled the qualities of Unconditional Excellence. More than just modeling it, Bess has actively cared—she has loved—by sponsoring her peers to aim high in their growth. She challenges others to aim high and then helps them achieve that high standard. She continues to do this with little thought for how she will benefit. She has lived the humble life and used her strengths for the benefit of others.

In one session, we asked everyone in the room to write a statement that they wanted read at their retirement party. As they read their announcements aloud, it amazed me that more than half of the people in that room thanked Bess for investing in them by sponsoring, mentoring, coaching, or simply by listening.

As each person read, I watched Bess' face. By the third mention of her name in her peers' retirement statements, she became teary-eyed. I also saw something else. The stunned expression on Bess' face told me she had no idea she had been that influential. She had invested so much into so many lives, yet she had obviously not thought to take credit or keep a long memory. She just did it and carried on with her life.

As I listened and observed, I kept thinking about what a powerful, meaningful reward it was for her to hear her peers— and former peers who had been promoted above her—honor her excellence.

After the final retirement announcement, the CEO said, "Bess is the finest example of giving her best for others that I have ever seen. She gives and in return she receives—even though she never asks for any return. That is what this company was founded on, and that is what I hope we maintain as a principle for generations of employees to come. I also hope every one of our employees, including me, live up to the standards that Bess has set. Thank you, Bess."

What an incredible connection! It is through our giving that the real power of Unconditional Excellence will be released. We can be very good at what we do, even outstanding, but it will be Unconditional Excellence only if it is based on a much greater motivation than personal gain. We have to love. We need to care about the people we work with.

Bess became successful because she was willing to share the best she had *with no conditions attached*. She did the right thing for the good of others, not worrying about herself and always putting the company's welfare first. By putting the company first—which certainly honors God—Bess worked quietly to make champions of others.

She did it by quietly expressing her best; she did it by caring. She loved.

Paul Tagliabue, the commissioner of the National Football League, was profiled on his leadership response to the tragedy of September 11, 2001. What struck me about the profile was how powerfully he made it clear that he cared about the people he worked with. While he was only one leader of many who rose to the occasion after September 11, what made him unique was that Paul Tagliabue was never considered a particularly warm or personal leader. He was one of the most effective and focused task leaders, not necessarily a leader you would characterize as caring and approachable.

Why did it take a tragedy like an attack on America for a leader to let his people know he cared? I imagine Paul Tagliabue has always cared. I also imagine that because he was uncomfortable showing it, he came across as an efficient leader, focused on the business he ran instead of the people he led. Businesses are just a collection of people. Caring about them and letting them know is what businesses should do naturally.

The Heart of the Matter

Out of the motivation of our hearts comes the power to live with excellence. I have written this book to help you apply these principles in the midst of the tumult of the marketplace. These principles work in any situation or circumstance. They wouldn't be godly principles if they didn't apply to every religion, to every nationality or culture, and every occupation. Excellence starts when we aim high, encourage others to do the same, and when love motivates us.

At the heart of these principles is both a decision and a challenge: "What will my legacy be?" I like that word *legacy*. It speaks of something more permanent than our transient lives. It connects us to the past and ties us to the future. If the only legacy I am concerned about is the one that my offspring will carry out, then I miss the opportunity to make a difference in hundreds, possibly even thousands, of lives.

In the story of Bess, no one said it quite this simply, but I can't think of a better tribute to people like her in the marketplace of whom people say, "She loved others and her caring actions demonstrated that." When we love, it motivates us to aim high and to encourage others to set higher goals.

Earlier in this book I wrote about personal destiny. I have come to realize that Unconditional Excellence is both the destination for people who want to leave a godly legacy and the path that leads us to it.

We *become* Unconditionally Excellent by *being* Unconditionally Excellent.

It's both a journey and a goal. It is attainable.

Index